DEFEND
CONFIDENTLY

DEFEND
CONFIDENTLY

**Elevate Situational Awareness
Secure Your Personal Safety
and Master Concealed Carry**

Stephen R. Mazzagatti

Published by Best Seller Publishing®, St. Augustine, FL
Best Seller Publishing® is a registered trademark.
Printed in the United States of America.

ISBN: 978-1966395300

This publication is designed to provide accurate and authoritative information with regard to the subject matter covered. It is sold with the understanding that the publisher is not engaged in rendering legal, accounting, or other professional advice. If legal advice or other expert assistance is required, the services of a competent professional should be sought. The opinions expressed by the author in this book are not endorsed by Best Seller Publishing® and are the sole responsibility of the author rendering the opinion.

For more information, please write:
Best Seller Publishing®
1775 US-1 #1070
St. Augustine, FL 32084
or call 1 (626) 765-9750

Visit us online at: www.BestSellerPublishing.org

Disclaimer

This book is not legal advice. This book expresses the opinion of the author, is based on his training and experience, and is provided solely for informational purposes. The views expressed are those of the author alone. The reader is responsible for his or her own actions. Adherence to all applicable laws and regulations, including federal, state, and local, including use of force for self-defense, firearm possession, transfer, carrying, purchasing, transporting, and all other aspects of firearm ownership in the United States, or any other jurisdiction, is the sole responsibility of the purchaser or reader. Many of the recommendations are general in nature and based on the author's personal training and experience. However, decisions and actions at any given moment should be based upon your own situation, depending on the events unfolding, your training and experience, and all applicable laws and regulations at that time. Neither the author, Martell Training Group, LLC, nor the publisher assumes any responsibility or liability whatsoever on behalf of the purchaser or reader of these materials.

Dedication

To Olivia and Emilie. While reaching for the stars,
remember the journey and stay safe along the way.

Unlock Your Exclusive Self-Defense Bonuses

Congratulations on taking the first step to confidently defend yourself! As a special thank you for reading *Defend Confidently*, we're giving you exclusive access to valuable tools that will enhance your self-defense skills. Click below to claim your bonuses and take your journey to the next level. You've already invested in your safety—now it's time to build the confidence to protect it!

https://mtgsafety.com/

TABLE OF CONTENTS

INTRODUCTION

Are you new to firearms or concealed carry? Does the thought of carrying a concealed firearm make you feel uneasy? Do you have extensive experience with guns but little or no experience with concealed carry? Are you interested in learning about non-lethal self-defense methods for use in public and at home? Do you want to gain confidence while in public by mastering situational awareness and concealed carry techniques?

My name is Stephen Mazzagatti. I'm a retired New Jersey state trooper, a former NJ-Certified Paramedic, and currently a CPR/AED/First Aid instructor, NRA Instructor in multiple disciplines, and FAA Certified Commercial Pilot. I'd like to welcome you to *Defend Confidently: Elevate Situational Awareness, Secure Your Personal Safety, and Master Concealed Carry.*

Throughout my career in the New Jersey State Police, I have worked in various roles, including Field Operations as a uniformed road trooper, detective investigating Cyber Crimes and Internet Crimes Against Children (ICAC), commercial pilot in the Aviation Bureau flying medevac, executive transport, and search and rescue missions, and as Unit Supervisor in the Firearms Investigation Unit. My extensive experience as a state trooper and Mobile Intensive Care Unit Paramedic has taught me a great deal about safety and preventative measures, which I use daily to stay safe and aware of my surroundings. In today's world, it is not only prudent but also essential to take responsibility for your own safety and survival.

I am the founder of Martell Training Group, LLC, a company dedicated to providing comprehensive safety, security, and survival education through both online content and in-person training. I authored this book to share the invaluable lessons I've accumulated over the years, with the hope that others can benefit from this knowledge. This book sheds light on various aspects of our lives where we often find ourselves in dangerous or vulnerable situations. These scenarios can frequently be avoided with greater situational awareness and proper preparation for potential confrontations. By embracing the belief that "survival is a mindset," you can position yourself to significantly enhance your personal safety and survival skills.

The most effective strategy for winning a confrontation is to avoid it altogether. However, when avoidance is not possible, there are numerous non-lethal methods available for self-defense that will be discussed in detail. Additionally, if you are contemplating carrying a concealed handgun for the protection of yourself and your family in public, it is crucial to understand and adhere to the important moral, legal, and safety considerations associated with concealed carry. This guide will cover these aspects comprehensively to ensure everyone is well-informed and practiced in these critical areas.

I decided to write this book in response to the numerous questions and comments I've received over the years from individuals who are new to concealed carry and who seek guidance or direction. Additionally, this book aims to address the concerns of those who have inquired about how to stay safe in various situations, whether they are carrying concealed or not. I believe that upon completing this book, you will possess the information and resources necessary to develop your own routines for mastering situational awareness and concealed carry. This will ultimately promote safety and confidence, whether you are at home or in public. For information about our online courses, book bonuses, and recommended products, please visit https://mtgsafety.com/.

Let's get started!

Chapter 1

Embarking on Awareness Mastery

In an instant, everything can change. Are you ready to see the small signs that could save your life?

Understanding Situational Awareness

The first topic we need to address is the definition of *situational awareness*. This term frequently comes up when discussing personal safety in public spaces. Situational awareness involves being conscious of what is happening around you at any given moment. More specifically, it means understanding the surrounding environment and recognizing how information, events, and your actions can impact both immediate and future goals and objectives.

Consider these four key components: Awareness, Intuition, Mindset, and Boundaries.

Awareness: This refers to your general awareness of your surroundings. Being mentally prepared involves constantly observing and noticing your environment. There are different levels of awareness, and different situations require different ones. A low level of awareness typically occurs when you feel safe, such as when you're

at home relaxing and reading a book. A moderate level of awareness is necessary when you are in a familiar area but surrounded by
strangers. A high level of awareness is crucial in unfamiliar areas
that might be associated with crime, such as when you get lost in a
high-crime neighborhood.

Intuition: There are moments when you experience a sense
of discomfort or unease about a situation. These feelings, often referred to as your gut instincts, or your sixth sense, are important—
you should pay attention to them because they frequently indicate
that something may not be right. Trusting these intuitive signals can
help you navigate through uncertain scenarios more effectively. It's
worth noting that these instincts are a culmination of your past experiences and subconscious processing, providing you with valuable
insights even when you can't immediately pinpoint the cause. And
while police officers cannot use these gut instincts as the sole reason
to make an arrest or obtain a search warrant, embracing and re-
specting these inner warnings can serve as a crucial guide in making
more informed decisions and following a cautious approach.

Mindset: Your mindset and thought process are pivotal in navigating difficult circumstances. Cultivate a resilient and unwavering
attitude, reminding yourself, "I will not be a victim." Focus on the
steps necessary to endure and succeed. Remember, your mental outlook frequently determines your ability to survive. Survivability is
fundamentally a state of mind. By maintaining a positive and proactive approach, you can transform obstacles into opportunities for
growth. Understanding that challenges are temporary and attain-
able can empower you to stay committed and resourceful. Have a
warrior mindset!

Boundaries: Personal boundaries are the limits you set for
yourself to protect your well-being and integrity. When these
boundaries are crossed by someone or something, it's crucial to
have a predetermined strategy to address the situation. Establishing and maintaining these boundaries is essential for your mental

and emotional health, allowing you to navigate interactions and relationships more effectively. It's also important to communicate your boundaries clearly to others and be prepared to enforce them consistently. By doing so, you ensure that your needs and values are respected, fostering healthier and more respectful connections. Obviously, in a self-defense situation, you may not have an opportunity to communicate your boundaries but should be ready to execute your defense strategy.

Situational awareness helps us identify potential threats and make informed decisions quickly. Mental conditioning means developing a plan of action to use if you are confronted with certain situations. There is no one-size-fits-all approach, and you may need to change your response as the situation unfolds.

IN YOUR HOME

So, why should you prepare for an intruder? What exactly are your chances of being a victim of a home invasion? According to the FBI's national crime statistics, in 2022, an estimated 1.2 million violent crimes occurred in the United States. They stated that a violent crime happens every 25.6 seconds. Violent crimes include murder, rape, robbery, and aggravated assault. Additionally, there were an estimated 6.5 million property crimes in 2022, totaling 6,513,829 incidents. Property crimes include burglary, larceny theft, motor vehicle theft, and arson.

According to RAINN, the Rape, Abuse & Incest National Network, most sexual assaults occur at or near the victim's home. A U.S. Department of Justice study found that if you're home during a criminal entry, there's a one in four chance of becoming a victim of violence. Hopefully, you never experience this, but preparation is crucial. When people ask me why I carry a gun or why I have pepper gel mounted in my home, my response is simple: I don't expect to have a house fire either, but I have fire extinguishers. A gun is another tool for self-defense.

Let's talk about the psychology of criminal predators. It's important to understand that criminals look like everybody else. They don't always fit the stereotype of someone who has just been released from prison. Common characteristics of criminals include a lack of conscience or mercy, viewing niceness as weakness, having an extremely selfish attitude, and appearing non-threatening and innocent. They're constantly seeking criminal opportunities. If you look like a victim, they will certainly try to take advantage of you.

Mental conditioning involves preparing yourself for various scenarios. Reflect on your day-to-day activities and identify moments when you were vulnerable. For example, if you were distracted by your phone in a parking lot, acknowledge that you were at risk and plan to avoid such situations in the future. This kind of mental conditioning helps you stay prepared and reduce your vulnerability.

Consider this scenario: Someone knocks on your door, claiming their car broke down and their cell phone has died. If this occurs, do not open the door. Offer to call someone for them, but never let a stranger into your house. Criminals often use such tactics to gain entry and then force their way in. Similarly, be cautious of anyone claiming to be from a utility company without proper identification or prior notice. These incidents are not as common as they once were because public awareness has been heightened by employee identification displayed on uniforms and frequently observed official logos on company vehicles; however, they do still occur.

Consider these home scenarios as well: If your kitchen has a door to the backyard, you wouldn't expect to see a stranger there. If you do, it should put you on high alert. Even if that person claims to have a reason to be there, don't just accept what they say. Contractors will usually knock on the front door rather than use the back door unless told otherwise.

When it comes to self-defense at home, you may not always have immediate access to a firearm. Think about a scenario where you are making dinner, and someone kicks in your front door. What would you do? This is where non-lethal options like pepper gel come in handy. Mounting a larger canister of pepper gel near common areas, such as next to your fire extinguisher, ensures it's easily accessible in case of an emergency. Pepper gel reduces the risk of blowback compared with pepper spray and has a range of about 25 feet. It's effective in most cases, although it may not work as well on individuals under the influence of drugs or alcohol.

Additionally, non-lethal or less-than-lethal defense options include flashlights with sirens or strobe functions, Byrna launchers for launching pepper spray substances in projectile form, and conducted energy devices like Tasers. These tools provide effective alternatives to firearms and can be crucial in defending yourself and your family.

While a comprehensive book could be dedicated to the topic of home defense alone, here are several key areas to consider when thinking about home security and ensuring the safety of yourself and your family.

Doors, Windows, and Exterior

Most common exterior doors can be kicked in with little effort. For about $100, you can buy a reinforcement kit to add to your door frame and locking areas. Many of these kits can be added on without removing your door and take about 30 minutes to install. This can give you valuable time to get to your safe room or self-defense weapon.

Make a list of all your doors and windows and go through each one to make sure they can easily open and lock properly. For a low cost, you can buy additional locking mechanisms for windows and doors, such as a security bar for any sliding doors.

Trim exterior shrubs and bushes close to your house to prevent hiding spots. Make sure you install motion LED lighting around your home and provide a lighted walkway to prevent dark or dimly lit areas.

Consider purchasing and installing wireless cameras and lights. You can hire an electrician or do it yourself. Many can be set up to detect motion and record on a cloud storage device for retrieval anytime. In addition, programmable lights for interior and exterior areas can give the appearance of someone being home. A simple Ring camera doorbell can allow you to "answer" your door remotely without having to place yourself in the vulnerable position of slightly opening the door to speak with the person standing there. Remember, some criminals wait for the opportunity to push open your door and force themselves inside once you unlock and open it, even slightly.

Consider getting an alarm system installed if you don't have one. If you can't afford an alarm system, purchase alarm signs for your yard. Many criminals will bypass a home if they think they will need to address an alarm system. Also, consider purchasing "Beware of the Dog" signs even if you don't have any pets. If you live alone, put a large pair of boots or pet bowls on the back porch or deck to give the appearance that a large man and pets reside at the residence as well.

Visit https://mtgsafety.com/ to see recommended products discussed in the book.

General Precautions

Don't announce on social media that you are going on vacation or out of town. Have a neighbor keep an eye on your house and property. Some police departments will conduct periodic property checks for residents when they are out of town. Check with your police department to see if they will do this when you aren't going to be home for a while.

Have a go bag containing a bleeding control kit, first aid kit, important papers, cash, a three-day supply of medication, and any personal items.

Have an alternate escape plan if you can't exit out of your front or rear doors. If you live on the second floor, you can purchase an emergency escape ladder to exit a window in case of a fire or intruder.

Safe Room

This is a specially designated room, ideally equipped with an alternate exit or escape route. It can be any room in your house, such as an office, spare bedroom, or storage space, but it should be easily accessible during an emergency, like in the event of a nighttime intruder. The door should be reinforced with deadbolt locks and additional locking mechanisms such as the Fliplock device, which is commonly used in school security. These devices are relatively inexpensive and can be installed on classroom doors. Easily engaged by a teacher or student, they significantly increase door security, preventing unwanted entry.

Your safe room should be stocked with essential supplies, including a flashlight, cell phone, portable power bank, spare charging cord, go bag, first aid kit, bleeding control kit, and a self-defense weapon. Options for self-defense include a firearm, pepper gel, Taser, or even a baseball bat.

The primary purpose of the safe room is to provide a secure space where you can stay safe in the event of an intruder. Once inside, you can retrieve a weapon and contact the authorities. If you believe the intruder is aware of your presence, you can shout, "I have a gun. Don't come near me," to deter them.

There are many tools available for home defense other than firearms. However, if you are considering a firearm for home defense, there are some key elements to consider.

Selecting a Firearm for Home Defense

When selecting a firearm, the first consideration should be its purpose. In this section, we'll discuss choosing a gun for home defense. We'll cover concealed carry in Chapter 4. For home defense, you need to consider factors such as power, functional reliability, revolver versus semi-automatic, size, caliber, new versus used, import versus domestic, and potential modifications, including aftermarket parts and accessories.

It's crucial to balance power with the risk of over-penetration. Different types of ammunition offer various performance characteristics. Many people don't realize that in stressful self-defense situations, a shotgun loaded with birdshot might be a better choice for home defense than a handgun. Shotguns provide a wider range to hit the target, which can be advantageous for those experiencing an adrenaline rush and who may not be very accurate with a handgun. Additionally, certain handgun ammunition can easily penetrate walls, posing a risk to other family members in adjacent rooms or even nearby neighbors.

When considering semi-automatic firearms versus revolvers, there are distinct pros and cons associated with each type. Semi-automatic firearms typically offer greater ammunition capacity compared to revolvers of a similar size. However, they are more prone to malfunctions. On the other hand, revolvers are known for their reliability, and they malfunction very infrequently in comparison with semi-automatic pistols. However, revolvers usually carry less ammunition and take more time to reload. Additionally, revolvers tend to be slightly bulkier than semi-automatics of comparable size.

Many people appreciate the extreme reliability of revolvers in self-defense situations. For instance, during my time as a road trooper, I carried a Smith & Wesson Model 640 revolver as a backup handgun. My recommendation is to try out both types of firearms to determine which one suits you best. Remember, if you choose a semi-automatic, it is crucial to be skilled in clearing any malfunctions. In an emergency, if your gun malfunctions when you pull the trigger, you must know how to quickly resolve the issue and get it functioning again.

For home defense, I often recommend a shotgun because it allows you to maintain a safer distance while still effectively hitting your target. Accessibility is another critical factor. If you live alone and are concerned about self-defense, you might want to keep a firearm nearby when you sleep. If you have children, it's essential to keep firearms locked in a safe and store them unloaded to prevent unauthorized access. Personal situations vary, but the utmost priority is ensuring firearms are not accessible to children or unauthorized individuals.

Some people choose to stage guns around their house, but I am not a proponent of this practice, especially if you have children. As a retired state trooper, I was trained to keep firearms either on my person or securely stored. Leaving a loaded or semi-loaded gun around the house was not advisable. For example, having a semi-automatic with a magazine inserted but no round in the chamber may offer a slight safeguard, as children may lack the strength to rack the slide. However, in a self-defense scenario, needing to rack the slide could be a significant disadvantage.

For home defense, I rely on an alarm system and pets to provide early warnings of intruders. Therefore, having a loaded gun by my bedside is not a primary concern for me. Depending on your circumstances, such as living alone or in a high-crime area, however, you might want to always keep a loaded gun closer to you.

When selecting a firearm for reliability, I recommend well-known commercial brands like Glock, Sig Sauer, Smith & Wesson, Remington, and Springfield Armory. All of these brands have proven themselves to be reliable, and parts are readily available. Avoid purchasing used firearms unless you know their history and maintenance records. Reliability is paramount; you don't want a cheaper, less reliable gun to malfunction when you need it most. I have carried Sig Sauer and

Glock firearms for nearly 30 years with minimal issues, and I trust their performance based on my extensive experience. I know there are many other reliable guns available, and you should consult with a reputable dealer or firearm instructor for recommendations.

When it comes to modifications, I prefer to keep my home defense and concealed carry firearms unaltered. I avoid adding numerous accessories, such as lights or optics, to maintain simplicity. Although I have no issues with enhancing guns used for range shooting or recreational purposes, I believe that simplicity is crucial for self-defense and home defense. In a later section, we will delve deeper into the topic of concealed carry and why I adhere to this minimalist approach.

Regarding ammunition, the first consideration is the type and caliber suitable for your firearm, which can be found in the user manual and stamped on the gun barrel or slide. Different ammunition types, such as jacketed hollow point (JHP) and full metal jacket (FMJ), offer various performance characteristics. JHP rounds expand on impact, reducing the risk of over-penetration, making them ideal for concealed carry and home defense. FMJ rounds, on the other hand, have higher penetration potential and are less suitable for these purposes.

Testing your chosen ammunition at the range is essential to ensure it performs well with your firearm. Additionally, consider changing out your ammunition periodically, especially if it is exposed to extreme conditions. Store ammunition in a cool, dry place to extend its lifespan. Although ammunition can last for decades, its performance can degrade under harsh conditions, so adjust your replacement schedule accordingly.

In summary, selecting a firearm for home defense involves considering various factors, including reliability, accessibility, available ammunition, and ease of use.

To access my YouTube channel for videos on Firearms Safety, visit the Book Bonuses Page at https://mtgsafety.com/

In Public

When you are in public, here are some key areas to consider and what your mindset should be to ensure your safety. First, it's crucial to maintain a heightened level of alertness while in public. For instance, when walking down a street, you should be observant of people in front of you, beside you, and behind you. You can simply periodically turn your head from side to side to see who's around you. Additionally, remain vigilant about individuals across the street who may have their eyes on you. Resist the temptation to look at your cell phone or become distracted while walking or waiting for a traffic light to change. If you're preoccupied, you may not notice someone following or watching you from across the street and slightly behind you.

ATMs

Automated teller machines (ATMs) come with specific challenges, primarily because you're withdrawing cash in a public setting, making you a tempting target, and focusing on using the machine can distract you from other people around you. It's crucial, therefore, to always remain vigilant about your surroundings. Whenever possible, opt for ATMs located inside stores or use them during daylight hours, which provides better visibility. Avoid using ATMs at night or in secluded areas to minimize potential risks. Additionally, refrain from standing around to handle your cash; secure it promptly. If you notice someone watching or approaching you, be prepared to leave the area quickly.

Elevators

Before stepping onto an elevator, there are two essential precautions to observe. Firstly, ensure that the elevator car is present. Although rare, malfunctions can occur where the doors open without the car being there. If you are distracted by your phone or engaged in conversation, you might unknowingly walk into an open shaft. Secondly, take note of who is already inside the elevator. If you feel uneasy about any individual, refrain from entering. Trust your instincts instead of rationalizing your discomfort. It's always safer to wait a bit longer than to risk being in an enclosed space with someone potentially dangerous.

If you do find yourself already inside an elevator and someone makes you feel threatened or uncomfortable, press the button for the next floor to exit immediately. Avoid using the emergency button as it typically stops the elevator, which could prolong your time in an unsafe situation.

Your Vehicle

There are numerous ways to stay safe and maintain situational awareness while in your vehicle. Always be vigilant about anyone lurking underneath or near your vehicle as you approach it in a parking garage or lot. If possible, park in well-lit areas or spots with high activity for better visibility. Scan the area to ensure no one is following or watching you. Have your keys or fob ready before you reach your vehicle to minimize the time spent unlocking it. You can also have pepper gel or a conducted energy device readily accessible.

If someone is nearby and appears to be observing your actions, avoid unlocking your car from a distance because this can reveal your vehicle's location. Instead, consider heading toward another aisle of cars and then move quickly to your vehicle at the last minute. This can hide your true target location and stop the other person blocking your path, for example.

Once inside your vehicle, immediately lock your doors and start the engine in case you need to leave swiftly. While driving, refrain from using your cell phone; not only is it illegal in most states, it's also distracting, diverting your attention from your situation and preventing you from being ready to react. Always wear your seatbelt, monitor your speed, and avoid tailgating. Ensure you always have an escape route, whether driving or when stopped in traffic. You do this by maintaining a sufficient distance from the vehicle ahead of you. While stopped in traffic, if you can clearly see the rear tires of the vehicle in front of you making contact with the pavement, this space should provide a necessary buffer, allowing for an effective escape route if the need arises.

While in traffic, get in the habit of performing slow scans from your side mirrors to your rearview mirror and back. If you notice someone approaching your vehicle, be prepared to drive away. Try to stay in a lane that provides an exit option while in stop-and-go traffic. Frequently check your rearview mirror for approaching people or vehicles.

In addition, you need to get the "whole picture" while driving, including looking ahead. For example, if you see some activity in the road ahead, such as protesters blocking the passage of cars, you can execute a U-turn and avoid potential confrontation. It may not be something that requires avoiding the area completely but something that requires slowing down, moving over, and caution, such as police or tow truck activity.

In addition, avoid driving behind utility trucks or any vehicle that seems to have unsecured loads. I've seen fatal collisions due to debris falling from these utility vehicles.

Road Rage

I strongly advise against engaging in any form of driving confrontations. Such actions can lead to severe consequences, including collisions. Moreover, you can never be sure if the other driver is armed or has a dangerous or violent history. I understand that your vehicle feels like your personal space, and when someone cuts you off or makes a rude gesture, it feels invasive and personal. However, it's crucial not to react or escalate the situation.

If you suspect that you are being followed, make a few consecutive right turns. If the vehicle remains behind you and you feel threatened, drive to the nearest well-lit area, police station, or any place where there are other people. Don't hesitate to call 911 from your cell phone for assistance.

In the unfortunate event that you find yourself needing to confront someone, try to leave the area immediately. If you cannot leave, ensure your doors are locked. Consider carrying pepper gel or mace if it is legal in your state. For instance, in New Jersey, you are allowed to carry up to three-quarters of an ounce of pepper spray. While conducted energy devices such as Tasers are also legal to possess in New Jersey, the law still restricts what can be carried outside your home for self-defense. Check with your state or local authorities before carrying anything for self-defense.

Distracted Driving

There's an abundance of information on the dangers of distracted driving, and in many states, it's illegal to use your cell phone without hands-free operation while driving. In New Jersey, this is considered a primary offense, meaning that police can pull you over solely for using your phone, even if you appear to be driving safely.

"Move Over" Laws

Many states have enacted some form of "Move Over" law. In New Jersey, this law was established following the tragic death of Trooper Marc Castellano. He was killed in the line of duty by a distracted driver who drifted onto the shoulder of the highway where Castellano was investigating a reported armed kidnapping suspect. This tragic incident underscores the importance of these laws.

Whenever you see any activity on the shoulder or the right lane, it's crucial to move over if possible. If you can't move over, slow down and employ a technique known as "Cover Your Brake." This involves placing your foot over the brake pedal and being prepared to brake immediately, reducing reaction time.

According to the National Highway Traffic Safety Administration (NHTSA), most fatal car accidents occur within 25 miles of home. For nonfatal accidents, more than half (52 percent) happen within 5 miles of home, and around 77 percent take place within 15 miles of a driver's home.

Other studies reported by the NHTSA showed similar findings: approximately 52 percent of all car accidents occur within a 5-mile radius of home, and 69 percent of all collisions happen within a 10-mile radius of home.

Because most fatal and serious accidents occur close to home, be particularly cautious in familiar areas where you may become complacent. As a paramedic, I've observed that fewer serious and fatal accidents tend to happen on days with bad weather compared to bright, sunny days. My theory is that during inclement weather, people are more cautious and vigilant, whereas, on clear, beautiful days, they may become complacent and less attentive. Exercise caution on these trips.

I also have a YouTube channel dedicated to Driving Safety Tips. To get access, visit https://mtgsafety.com/

The OODA Loop

One highly effective method to enhance situational awareness, widely used by the military and law enforcement, is the OODA Loop. OODA stands for Observation, Orientation, Decision, and Action. This decision-making framework consists of four stages that help individuals navigate potentially dangerous situations with greater clarity and responsiveness. Let's see an example in action:

Imagine you are walking on a street. By being aware of your surroundings—people in front of you, beside you, and behind you—you might notice someone across the street who appears to be watching you. This is the **observation** phase. Next, you **orient** yourself by considering your position and available options. In this orientation phase, you assess the potential threat and how it aligns with your personal boundaries and safety protocols.

Based on your orientation, you decide, "If he crosses the street, I'm going to enter the busy store up ahead," or "If he gets too close, I'll be ready to use my pepper gel." This is the **decision** phase, where you formulate a clear plan of action. Finally, you execute your decision. If the individual crosses the street or invades your personal space, you proceed with your predetermined response, whether it's seeking safety in a crowded area or using a self-defense tool. This constitutes the **action** phase.

The OODA Loop provides a framework for a continuous and dynamic process that mirrors the ongoing nature of decision-making and the necessity to adapt swiftly in self-defense situations. Each phase seamlessly feeds into the next, allowing for stages to be repeated or skipped as the situation demands. Utilizing the OODA Loop ensures you maintain a high level of situational awareness and are prepared to act decisively and effectively.

Training Your Mind for Awareness: Techniques to Become More Aware of Your Surroundings

Enhancing your observation skills is crucial for becoming more attuned to your environment. Here are some techniques to help you hone your observation skills and become more aware of your surroundings:

Mindful awareness: Practice mindful awareness to stay fully present and engage in the current moment both within yourself and in the world around you. This practice is characterized by an attitude of curiosity, acceptance, and a deliberate choice to observe without judgment or immediate reaction. It promotes a focus on the here and now, allowing individuals to prioritize what truly matters to them while setting aside distracting thoughts and emotions.

Active listening: Focus on listening more intently during conversations and in your daily environment. This could mean tuning into background noises, the tone of someone's voice, or even the silence in a room.

Note-taking: Carry a small notebook to jot down observations throughout the day. Writing things down can help reinforce your memory and make you more conscious of your surroundings.

Sensory engagement: Fully experience your environment by engaging all your senses. Touch different textures, smell various scents, and observe the play of light and shadows to deepen your sensory awareness. Sensory engagement serves as the primary conduit or way through which we gather information about our environment. This kind of exploration is the initial step in our cognitive development, forming the groundwork for our understanding of the world.

By being mindful and paying attention to our senses, we can gain a deeper understanding of our experiences and the world around us.

Change your routine: Alter your daily routine or take a different route to work. This can help you break out of autopilot mode and make you more observant of new details. I do this frequently. It can help you avoid complacency, something that can happen to all of us.

Practice sketching: Drawing or sketching scenes from your environment can enhance your ability to notice and remember details. It doesn't have to be perfect art; the act of sketching itself sharpens your observation skills.

By incorporating these techniques into your daily life, in addition to boosting your observational skills to help keep yourself safe, you can also improve your ability to notice and appreciate the world around you, leading to a richer and more engaged experience of life. This is especially important in today's world of electronic devices that seem to consume our attention.

Overcoming Common Barriers

Complacency happens when we get into a routine and assume that since nothing has happened, most likely, nothing will happen in the future. Because we don't anticipate danger, we don't take necessary precautions to ensure our safety.

As a retired state trooper, I possess firsthand knowledge of how easily one can fall into the trap of complacency, especially after countless routine interactions with the public. The temptation to take shortcuts when pressed for time can be overwhelming. For instance, one might neglect the crucial step of calling in a vehicle stop on the radio before contacting the driver. As a matter of procedure, police call in their stops on the radio, providing detailed information about the vehicle, registration, driver, and location. If you don't respond or "check in" after a certain period, the dispatcher will send other officers to check on you. They will also have information to investigate if they need to follow up. Since most vehicle stops are routine, the temptation might be to skip this step to make a "quick stop"—but then if something goes wrong, no one back at the station will know where you are or have any leads as to the last person you were in contact with.

Another example is parking your patrol car on the side of the road to complete paperwork. If you don't expect anyone to approach, you might keep your head down while completing paperwork. However, some law enforcement officers have been ambushed this way. An unexpected knock on your window from someone merely seeking directions can serve as a powerful reminder. It underscores the importance of staying vigilant and not allowing oneself to be caught off guard. Such experiences reinforce the vital lesson that in police work, complacency can have serious consequences. You can adopt this mindset as well.

Driving the same route home each night can lead to complacency. It's easy to become less vigilant when you consistently follow the same path without incident. Sometimes, you might find yourself arriving home with little or no recollection of the drive. This should be a clear indication that you were either distracted or not fully paying attention.

Distractions can significantly disrupt situational awareness. Therefore, it is crucial to minimize distractions that could impair your awareness at any given moment, especially in this era dominated by electronic devices. For instance, I've observed numerous individuals engrossed in their phones while waiting for traffic lights to change, walking on the street, and standing in line at checkout counters.

In the state police academy, the instructors employed a particularly intense method during car stop scenarios. They would covertly position themselves nearby and, at a pivotal moment, surprise the recruit who was engaged with the driver by discharging a shotgun loaded with blanks. The deafening blast, combined with the unexpected shock, served as a powerful lesson about the importance of maintaining constant situational awareness.

Encountering stressful and high-pressure scenarios can diminish your capacity to remain vigilant and attentive to your surroundings. Therefore, mastering stress management techniques is crucial to maintaining awareness and focus. Adopting strategies to handle stress effectively not only helps in staying composed but also enhances overall mental well-being. By integrating relaxation methods, time management skills, and regular physical activity into your routine, you can better navigate stressful environments and maintain a balanced state of mind.

Maintaining a Calm and Focused Mindset: Strategies to Stay Composed and Alert Under Pressure

For law enforcement personnel, this training begins at the academy on the very first day. Personally, at the New Jersey State Police Academy, I was thrust into a world of relentless stress for nearly six months.

Academy instructors were constantly in our faces, scrutinizing our every move. The intention behind this high-pressure environment is to assess how recruits perform under extraordinary stress. Whether it was during meals, marching to class, or being abruptly awakened at night to perform unscheduled tasks, the pressure seemed endless. During all this, we had to successfully complete academic courses, meet physical fitness standards, pass firearm qualifications, and demonstrate water safety and survival skills. The rigorous training ensures that only those best suited for high-stress environments are entrusted with the profound responsibility of carrying a firearm and potentially taking away someone's liberty or life.

Many recruits do not make it through, which underscores the demanding nature of the academy. However, not everyone can attend a police academy or enlist in the military, and therefore, they may not be accustomed to such high levels of stress in their daily lives. But for those who carry concealed handguns to protect themselves and their families, the ability to remain calm and focused under pressure is especially crucial.

But even without carrying a weapon, staying calm and focused under pressure is essential for managing stress and performing effectively. Here are some strategies to help you remain composed and alert in challenging situations:

- **Controlled breathing and meditation:** Practice deep, slow breathing to help calm your nervous system and reduce stress. You can also try mindful meditation or yoga. Engaging in mindfulness and meditation can significantly boost your awareness and help you stay present in the moment. Mindfulness encourages you to focus on the present by observing your thoughts, feelings, and sensations without judgment. This practice can be as simple as paying attention to your breath, noting the rise and fall of your chest, and feeling the air pass through your nostrils. Meditation, on the other hand, often involves a more structured approach, where you might sit quietly, close your eyes, and concentrate on a particular object, mantra, or visualization. This practice can help calm your mind and bring a sense of peace. By incorporating various exercises, you can cultivate a deeper sense of presence and attentiveness in your daily life. These practices can help you stay grounded and present, reducing anxiety and improving concentration.

- **Regular stress training:** Consistent practice in stressful environments can help you become more accustomed and resilient to pressure. Talk to a firearm instructor about stress training at your range. You can perform simple exercises to increase your heart rate during typical training to simulate a stressful situation. You then perform some self-defense techniques or exercises and see how well you perform under stress.

- **Mental rehearsal and visualization:** Mentally go through your tasks and actions to ensure you are prepared for any situation. Envision successful outcomes and rehearse scenarios in your mind to build confidence and preparedness.

- **Physical fitness:** Maintain a regular exercise routine to keep your body in peak condition, which can help reduce stress and improve focus. In addition, a balanced diet and adequate sleep are essential for maintaining mental and physical health. These habits can enhance your ability to handle stress and stay alert.

- **Support systems and positive self-talk:** Rely on trusted colleagues, friends, or family members to provide emotional support and guidance. Replace negative thoughts with positive affirmations. Remind yourself of your strengths and past successes. Positive self-talk can boost your confidence and keep you focused. Remember, survival is a mindset!

- **Time management:** Organize your tasks and priorities to avoid feeling overwhelmed and to maintain control over your environment. Creating a simple schedule to follow for the next day can go a long way in reducing stress.

- **Focus on what you can control and develop problem-solving skills:** Accept that some factors are beyond your control. Concentrate on what you can manage and influence, and let go of what you cannot change. Enhance your problem-solving abilities by practicing different strategies and approaches. Being adept at finding solutions can reduce stress and increase your confidence in handling pressure. As a simple example, you can't control whether someone cuts you off in traffic, but you *can* control how you respond.
- **Reflect and learn:** After facing a stressful situation, take time to reflect on what happened and what you can learn from it. Understanding your responses and identifying areas for improvement can prepare you better for future challenges. I learned this early on as a pilot. You are taught to evaluate every takeoff and approach to landing and think about what can be improved for next time because conditions such as weather and aircraft configuration change constantly.

By incorporating these strategies into your daily routine, you can build resilience and maintain a calm and focused mindset, even in high-pressure situations.

During my residency at the New Jersey State Police Academy, we encountered a multitude of scenarios designed to develop our skills and prepare us for whatever the job could throw at us. But this was done not simply by putting us in a range of different situations to let us practice dealing with them in a safe environment. After all, no training can anticipate everything that might happen. So, in addition, training focused on developing skills and mindsets that could be applied to pretty much every situation. That way, we would be prepared even if we hadn't faced something in a drill.

I distinctly remember one instructor who excelled at creating a comfortable environment during informal training exercises. He would converse with us as colleagues rather than berating us as recruits. Just when we had grown accustomed to his friendly demeanor, he would suddenly shift his tone and attitude, beginning to yell at the slightest provocation. Later, I understood that this approach was designed to teach us a crucial lesson: no matter how calm and uneventful a situation might appear, it could change in an instant, and we needed to be prepared for that.

Now that you have a foundational understanding of situational awareness, it's time to delve deeper into the practice of vigilance. In the next chapter, we'll explore how to make vigilance your first line of defense in any situation.

Chapter 2

VIGILANCE: YOUR
FIRST DEFENSE

The best way to win a confrontation is to avoid it. However, even with the best intentions in the world, that is sometimes simply not possible. Imagine walking on a dimly lit street; you may be lost, your senses heightened, every shadow a potential threat. It's in moments like these that vigilance becomes your greatest ally. Vigilance, often overlooked, is the cornerstone of personal safety and defense. In this chapter, we'll explore how to sharpen your awareness and stay one step ahead of danger.

Maintaining a vigilant mindset can be the crucial difference between safety and danger. In essence, if you're prepared, you can respond effectively instead of being caught off guard and at a disadvantage. Being prepared encompasses various facets of personal safety and survival. This preparation includes learning and practicing proper self-defense techniques, purchasing appropriate weapons for home defense and personal carry, and having essential equipment on hand, such as an individual first aid kit or bleeding control kit. But, in addition, there's a psychological component regarding how the brain processes threats, which can be key to dealing safely with a situation. Even better, because the knowledge is in your brain, you never have to worry about leaving these techniques at home.

Understanding how the brain interprets threats is essential in recognizing why staying alert can be crucial for our safety. The human brain is wired to detect potential dangers quickly, a survival mechanism that has evolved over millennia. This innate response is primarily managed by the amygdala, a small, almond-shaped cluster of nuclei located deep within the temporal lobe.

According to the Encyclopedia Britannica, the amygdala is one of the components of the limbic system, which, in addition to memory formation, is responsible for the control of emotions and behavior.

When a threat is perceived, the amygdala sends distress signals to other parts of the brain, initiating the "fight or flight" response. This reaction prepares the body to either confront the danger or escape it by initiating a series of physiological changes such as increased heart rate, heightened senses, and the release of adrenaline. These changes enable us to respond swiftly to potential hazards.

Experiencing a certain level of fear can be beneficial because it prompts you to either confront a danger or evade it effectively. However, excessive fear can become debilitating and prevent you from taking necessary actions. This concept is analogous to the experience of police officers with paranoia. A moderate amount of paranoia can enhance their safety and vigilance, but an overwhelming degree can hinder their ability to perform their duties effectively.

Your responses will be influenced by your personal experiences, your capacity to confront and manage the perceived threat, and any relevant training you may have undergone.

Vigilance allows us to respond more effectively to these signals. In modern society, threats might not always be physical; they can also be psychological or situational, such as navigating a high-stress work environment or dealing with social pressures. However, the last thing we want to do is escalate a situation in public because we've been under constant stress at work. By staying alert and aware of our surroundings and internal states, we can better manage stress and avoid risky situations.

In addition, cultivating mindfulness and situational awareness can enhance our ability to distinguish between real and perceived threats. This distinction is crucial because chronic stress and anxiety can arise from constantly feeling threatened by non-imminent dangers, which can have detrimental effects on mental health.

In essence, while our brain's threat detection system is a powerful tool for survival, it isn't perfect. Understanding and managing it through awareness and mindfulness can significantly improve our overall well-being and safety in both immediate and long-term contexts.

Let's take our earlier example of walking on a dimly lit street. Now, imagine you are a young woman named Sarah. One evening, as Sarah walks home from work, she finds herself on a dimly lit street she doesn't recognize. With each step, her senses heighten, and every shadow seems like a potential threat. She remembers reading about the importance of vigilance and decides to stay alert, scanning her surroundings for any unusual activity. As she turns a corner, she notices a figure lurking in the shadows. Her heart races, but her training in self-defense and her understanding of threat detection mechanisms kick in. She quickly evaluates her options and decides to cross to the other side of the street, maintaining eye contact with the figure to show she is aware of their presence. She also reaches for her pepper gel and keeps it firmly in her hand, ready to use. The figure hesitates and then disappears into an alley, leaving Sarah relieved yet more convinced of the importance of vigilance.

If we look at certain historical events, we can see they have repeatedly shown the value of being prepared and vigilant. Take, for instance, the events leading up to the attack on Pearl Harbor in 1941. Despite various warning signs, the lack of vigilance resulted in a devastating surprise attack. In contrast, during the Cuban Missile Crisis in 1962, heightened vigilance and careful monitoring allowed the U.S. to detect and respond to the Soviet Union's missile deployment in Cuba, ultimately averting a potential nuclear catastrophe. In both cases, the ability to anticipate and recognize threats played a crucial role in the outcome, underscoring the timeless lesson that the best way to win a confrontation is often to avoid it through preparedness and awareness.

As part of my annual in-service training as a state trooper, we would watch videos and analyze real-life incidents involving police officers from around the country. Typically, these incidents did not end well for the officers, and they were used as training tools to see what tactical errors were made and how to avoid the same mistakes. To this day, I still remember some of the most disturbing of these videos. After watching, I vowed to never let certain things happen to me or put myself in those same situations. In some cases, it was obvious that no preparation could have prevented the attack; however, the type and speed of the officer's response were critical in determining their survival. You can benefit from this type of training as well simply by imagining certain situations and what your response would be. When you watch or hear about an incident involving an attack, break it down as to how you may have reacted or if you could have been a victim if it were you in that situation.

In Chapter 1, Embarking on Awareness Mastery, we mentioned the importance of mental conditioning, which involves imagining your typical day and identifying situations where you might have been vulnerable. For instance, did you walk to your car while distracted by checking your phone for an email or text message? Did you sit in your car without immediately closing and locking the door while reading a text? Did you step onto an elevator without looking and then realize the only other occupant made you feel uneasy? These scenarios highlight potential exposures that you can address. By analyzing your daily routine, you can identify and rectify these vulnerabilities.

Next time you're walking to your car, stay vigilant and focus on getting to your car safely. Once inside, lock the door, start the engine, and then, if it's safe to do so, check your phone or attend to other tasks. If you're waiting for an elevator and the doors open to reveal someone who makes you feel unsafe, trust your instincts and don't get on. Your gut instinct is a powerful tool, and you should not rationalize it away.

It's crucial to periodically assess your daily activities to ensure you are not inadvertently putting yourself in harm's way. As part of your mental conditioning, it's equally important to visualize how you would respond to various emergency scenarios. Remember, survival is fundamentally a mindset!

Consider what you would do if someone suddenly walked in through your front door or forcefully kicked it in. Most doors, especially those without reinforcement, can be easily breached. This scenario is not far-fetched and can occur even when people are home. In fact, this has been reported recently in the news in Canada. Gangs of criminals have used crowbars to break into homes even when homeowners are present. Their goal has been to look for keys to steal their cars and any valuables they see. In some cases, the alarms were sounding, and it didn't affect the criminals. The police in Canada have even recommended residents leave their keys readily accessible for would-be burglars so they don't have to search for them when they break into their homes! This disturbing trend has happened in the town next to mine in New Jersey. There have been several break-ins by gangs of criminals to steal vehicles and valuables. Therefore, it is wise to have at least a mental plan for how you would react if someone attempted to enter your home through either the front or back door.

Many people do not anticipate someone approaching their back door. For example, my back door opens into my kitchen, so if I were preparing dinner and noticed someone there, it would immediately raise alarms. Other than the occasional visit from my neighbors searching for their cat, I rarely see anyone near my back door. Therefore, it's important to think through these various scenarios and determine your course of action.

Of course, I strongly advise against opening your back door unless you are certain of who is on the other side. For someone to come onto your property and approach your back door is highly unusual and inappropriate in most cases. We will explore some self-defense options later in the book, but for now, consider what actions you might take if your children are in another room when someone forcefully enters through either door. Have a plan.

DEVELOPING SITUATIONAL AWARENESS

Scanning Your Environment: Techniques for Observing Your Surroundings Without Appearing Suspicious or Overly Concerned

Being aware of your surroundings is crucial for staying safe and making informed decisions. However, it's important to do so in a way that doesn't draw unnecessary attention to yourself or raise suspicion. I do these things when I'm out in public every day. Here are some strategies to help you observe your environment discreetly:

1. **Practice situational awareness:** Always be mindful of your environment. This means paying attention to who and what is around you without fixating on any one thing for too long. Use your peripheral vision to gather information subtly.

2. **Blend in:** Dress and behave in a manner that suits the environment you're in. This helps you to avoid standing out. For example, if you're in a business district, wearing business attire will help you blend in. This is important for police work during surveillance. Typically, police don't use vehicles that look like police cars when conducting surveillance. They also don't wear uniforms. They dress and behave according to the environment.

3. **Casual scanning:** Instead of staring or making abrupt movements, scan your surroundings casually. Look around slowly and naturally, as if you're simply admiring the scenery or looking for a place to sit. This applies to when you're in your vehicle as well. Simply scan from mirror to mirror casually while waiting for traffic to move.

4. **Use reflections:** Utilize reflective surfaces like windows, mirrors, and even smartphone screens to observe what's happening around you without directly looking at people or events.

5. **Engage in a secondary activity:** Engage in an activity like checking your phone, reading a book, or sipping a drink while scanning your environment. This gives you a reason to look around without appearing suspicious.

6. **Position yourself strategically:** Choose a spot where you can see most of the area without being too conspicuous. Sitting at the back of a room or facing the entrance allows you to observe without constantly turning your head. It's always good practice to sit with your back to a wall and know where the nearest exit is located. This allows you to observe and exit immediately if necessary.

7. **Trust your instincts:** Pay attention to your gut feelings. If something feels off, it's worth taking a closer look. Your instincts are often your first line of defense. Remember the elevator scenario. Don't get on the elevator if the occupant or occupants make you feel uneasy.

By integrating these techniques into your daily routine, you can stay aware of your surroundings in a manner that is both effective and unobtrusive. This not only enhances your personal safety but also allows you to react promptly and appropriately should any unexpected situations arise.

Understanding Body Language: Techniques for Recognizing Non-Verbal Cues That Could Mean Danger

Understanding body language is a crucial skill for identifying potential dangers in your environment. By accurately reading non-verbal signals, you can detect threats before they fully materialize. This skill involves interpreting various forms of body language, including facial expressions, gestures, posture, and eye movements.

The first fundamental aspect to consider is facial expressions. The human face can convey a wide range of emotions, from happiness to anger and even fear. For instance, furrowed brows, clenched jaws, and tightened lips often indicate stress or aggression. Recognizing these signs early can provide you with the opportunity to de-escalate a situation or remove yourself from a potential threat. In most cases, it's easy to see if someone is upset by looking at their facial expressions.

Gestures are another vital component of body language. People often use their hands to express themselves, and certain movements can be telling. Rapid or exaggerated hand movements might suggest anxiety or agitation. Conversely, clenched fists or sudden, forceful gestures could indicate a readiness to engage in physical confrontation.

Posture also plays a significant role in non-verbal communication. An individual's stance can give you clues about their intentions. Someone who stands with a rigid, tense posture might be feeling defensive or aggressive. Someone who moves into a fighting stance is showing signs they are ready and willing to fight. On the other hand, a relaxed and open stance generally indicates a non-threatening demeanor.

Eye movements are perhaps one of the most revealing aspects of body language. Direct eye contact can suggest confidence or aggression, while avoiding eye contact might indicate discomfort or deceit. Rapid blinking or frequent glancing around could be signs of nervousness or an attempt to assess the environment for threats. I've observed that wide-open eyes, where you can see the whites of their eyes above and below their iris, can be a sign of anxiety or stress.

In addition to these primary indicators, it is crucial to consider the context and cultural background when interpreting body language. Different cultures have unique non-verbal communication styles, and understanding these nuances can greatly enhance your ability to accurately read people. For instance, as a detective, I have encountered individuals who avoided making eye contact. This behavior was not a sign of deception but rather a reflection of their cultural norm, where maintaining eye contact with an authority figure is considered disrespectful. Furthermore, always consider the specific situation and any known background information about the individuals involved.

Developing the ability to read body language effectively requires practice and keen observation. By honing this skill, you can better protect yourself and those around you by anticipating and mitigating potential threats before they escalate.

Recognizing Patterns: Identify Normal and Abnormal Patterns in Your Environment to Spot Danger Before It Materializes

By paying close attention to consistent and inconsistent activities in your environment, you can identify potential hazards before they become imminent. Maintaining a high level of awareness and keen observation skills allows you to enhance your safety and readiness.

You can hone your situational awareness by continuously asking yourself if anything appears different or out of place. For instance, if you routinely walk the same path to your vehicle and one day notice a van parked along the route, this anomaly should prompt you to consider the possibility that someone might be inside the van, potentially waiting for an unsuspecting victim to pass by. Additionally, take note of individuals sitting in parked cars. While they might be waiting for a friend or loved one, it is also possible that they could be waiting for their next target.

These days, I frequently notice individuals sitting idly in their cars, most likely engrossed in their phones as they await friends or family. Because their intentions remain uncertain, I maintain a vigilant attitude and trust my instincts to stay safe. As a matter of practice, I avoid walking by vehicles that have people inside, if possible. Additionally, I make it a point to highlight these observations to my children, encouraging them to cultivate awareness of their surroundings as well.

Numerous towns have embraced advanced crime prevention and response technologies, notably artificial intelligence (AI)-driven security systems. These systems can detect specific threats, such as the sound of gunshots, and even someone carrying a firearm, and promptly alert law enforcement authorities. This allows officers to swiftly respond to the precise location of the incident, enhancing community safety and reducing response times. Furthermore, integrating this approach with state-of-the-art technological innovations or enhancing community awareness can significantly amplify your capability to anticipate and counter potential threats. Utilizing advanced tools such as AI-driven analytics and real-time monitoring systems, in conjunction with promoting neighborhood watch programs, can establish a comprehensive framework for early threat detection and prevention.

This multifaceted strategy not only strengthens security but also cultivates a culture of collective responsibility and preparedness within the community.

Practical Exercises to Enhance Vigilance

Engaging in activities designed to enhance your ability to notice and remember details in busy environments can help sharpen your observational prowess, making you more attentive to your surroundings.

Consider focusing on small elements that often go unnoticed, such as the color of a passerby's shoes, the type of plants in a nearby garden, or the different sounds you hear in a crowded café. Over time, these exercises not only improve your attention to detail but also enrich your overall sensory awareness and cognitive abilities. The next time you enter a coffee shop, try to notice the people and activities around you. If someone asked you about the person standing behind you in line, could you describe them?

Mindfulness Practices: Techniques to Stay Present and Aware, Reducing Distractions and Improving Focus

In the summer of 1980, Dan Millman, a world-class gymnast, found himself at a crossroads. After a severe injury from an accident, his dreams of Olympic glory seemed shattered. Struggling with physical limitations and uncertainty, Dan discovered a new path through Socrates, a mysterious gas station attendant who introduced him to the way of the peaceful warrior. Socrates taught Dan the importance of mindfulness practices, techniques that emphasized staying present and aware, significantly reducing distractions, and improving focus.

Dan's journey, as detailed in *Way of the Peaceful Warrior,* is a testament to the transformative power of these practices. By learning to quiet his mind and be fully present in each moment, Dan not only rehabilitated his body but also found a deeper sense of peace and clarity. This shift in perspective was crucial as it helped him navigate the challenges ahead with resilience and honor. His story mirrors the experiences of many athletes, like Michael Jordan, who credited mindfulness and meditation for his unparalleled focus and success on the basketball court. Through these practices, Dan Millman and Michael Jordan exemplify how staying present can lead to profound personal and professional growth, emphasizing the timeless wisdom that true strength lies within the mind.

Staying focused and present can be challenging in our fast-paced world, especially with all the electronic devices, but mindfulness techniques offer valuable tools to help. By practicing mindfulness, you can minimize distractions and enhance your concentration. These techniques involve being fully aware of your thoughts, emotions, and surroundings in the present moment.

Like pretty much everyone, I experience days when I'm stressed or upset and don't fully understand why. Upon reflection, I can usually understand the source or origin and take steps to reduce or alleviate the stress. Sometimes, I park somewhere with privacy to think about my day. Whether through meditation, mindful breathing, or simply paying closer attention to daily tasks, these practices can significantly improve your mental clarity and productivity. Additionally, integrating mindfulness into your routine can lead to better stress management and overall well-being.

Scenario Training: Role-Playing Different Scenarios to Practice Vigilance and Quick Decision-Making Under Stress

Scenario training immerses participants in a variety of simulated situations, enhancing their ability to stay alert and make swift, effective decisions under pressure. This method is particularly beneficial for honing skills in real-world contexts, such as emergency response, law enforcement, and high-stakes business environments. By engaging in these practice scenarios, individuals can develop a heightened sense of awareness and improve their problem-solving capabilities.

A similar approach was a key component of training at the state police academy. It allowed instructors to observe firsthand how recruits handled different situations and whether they comprehended essential concepts. We never knew what the day or night would bring, and unlike the selection process, which involved sporadic assessments, living at the state police academy provided a controlled environment where instructors could increase stress and uncertainty at any time, day or night, to observe recruits' reactions. An applicant could look very capable during an interview or standalone evaluation, but nothing compared to living in a high-stress environment to gain a complete picture of how each recruit handled stress.

One of the key benefits of this type of training is that it allows participants to experience the stress and urgency of actual events in a controlled environment. This not only helps in building confidence but also ensures that they are better prepared to handle similar situations. The scenarios can be tailored to reflect specific challenges relevant to a particular field, making the training highly applicable and practical. For concealed carry individuals, you can create a shoot or no-shoot scenario based on the events that unfold. In addition, you can simulate a stressful environment, such as an increased heart rate and people screaming during the scenario, to observe how they respond.

Additionally, incorporating feedback and reflection sessions post-scenario can further enhance the learning experience. By analyzing their actions and decisions, participants gain valuable insights into their strengths and areas for improvement. This reflective practice encourages continuous growth that is essential for maintaining high performance in dynamic and unpredictable situations.

In addition to role-playing scenarios, you can simply imagine yourself in different scenarios and how you would react. For example, while waiting in line at a store, imagine if someone with a gun walked into the main entrance and started shooting. Where would you go? What would you do? Is there a place for you to run and protect yourself? What if two people behind you in line started arguing, and it escalated into a physical altercation? What would you do? I believe periodically thinking about various scenarios and possible outcomes keeps you vigilant and prepared for unexpected events.

On January 15, 2009, Captain Chesley "Sully" Sullenberger faced an unprecedented crisis when US Airways Flight 1549 struck a flock of geese, causing both engines to fail. Amid the chaos, Sully's observational skills and mindfulness practices came into play. He quickly noted specific details in the busy environment of airspace and New York City below him, such as the densely populated buildings and the Hudson River's open expanse with the many helicopters and ferries operating in the area. He was turning toward Teterboro Airport in New Jersey, but quickly realized that wasn't an option as he didn't have the necessary altitude to glide that distance. His ability to stay present and aware, a testament to his rigorous mindfulness practices, allowed him to reduce distractions and focus solely on the task at hand.

As the situation escalated, with a crash seeming inevitable, Sully engaged in scenario training, drawing on years of role-playing different emergencies to practice vigilance and quick decision-making under stress. He discussed this later, saying that for years, he practiced emergencies in flight simulators as required by regulations. As a commercial pilot myself, I know these simulator drills test pilots in various emergency situations and examine their responses. This training typically results in developing muscle memory, so when a similar event occurs in real life, you respond accordingly.

He communicated calmly with air traffic control and his crew, running through potential solutions until he determined that landing on the Hudson River was the safest option. His last transmission was, "We're gonna be in the Hudson." His decision-making under pressure, honed through countless hours of preparation, ultimately led to the successful water landing of Flight 1549. All 155 passengers and crew survived, showcasing how observation drills, mindfulness, and scenario training can collectively prepare individuals to handle even the most harrowing situations with precision and calmness.

In summary, scenario training is a powerful tool for developing vigilance and quick decision-making skills under stress. By simulating real-life challenges, it prepares individuals to respond effectively and confidently, ultimately leading to better outcomes in high-pressure environments.

Now that you've honed your vigilance, it's time to delve deeper into recognizing the subtle signs of danger. In the next chapter, we'll explore how to identify the often-overlooked cues that can alert you to potential threats before they escalate. Stay tuned for a deeper dive into spotting subtle danger signs.

Chapter 3

Spotting Subtle
Danger Signs

Imagine walking into a crowded room and immediately sensing something is off. Your instincts are screaming at you, but you can't quite put your finger on what's wrong. Perhaps you're tempted to ignore it, thinking your imagination is playing tricks on you, or you're being paranoid. But understanding these subtle signals can be the difference between safety and danger. This phenomenon is well-documented in Gavin de Becker's book, *The Gift of Fear: Survival Signals That Protect Us from Violence*, which emphasizes the importance of trusting one's intuition. De Becker recounts numerous real-life incidents where individuals sensed danger but ignored their instincts, often with dire consequences. Conversely, those who heeded their gut feelings frequently avoided potentially life-threatening situations.

One such example is the disturbing story of a woman named Kelly. One evening, Kelly was returning to her apartment when she noticed a man standing near the entrance. The man offered to help her carry her groceries, and despite feeling uneasy, Kelly accepted his help, rationalizing that she was being overly suspicious. Unfortunately, this decision led to a horrible ordeal where the man forced his way into her apartment and assaulted her. Kelly later recounted how her initial instinct was to refuse his help, but societal conditioning to be polite overrode her survival instinct. Remember the elevator scenario: don't get on if something or someone makes you feel uneasy.

In contrast, consider the story of a man named John, who was leaving a late-night meeting in an unfamiliar part of town. As he walked to his car, he felt a sudden, inexplicable sense of dread. Trusting his intuition, John immediately turned around and returned to the building, where he asked a security guard to escort him to his car. Later, it was discovered that a group of men had been waiting in the parking lot, most likely intending to rob him. John's decision to listen to his gut feeling potentially saved his life, illustrating the critical importance of trusting one's intuition, as highlighted by Gavin de Becker.

From my experience as a state trooper, I understand that law enforcement officers cannot rely solely on their "sixth sense" or gut feelings to justify an arrest or obtain a search warrant. However, they can, in fact, use their instincts or gut feelings to exercise increased caution or to approach a situation with heightened alertness when they might not otherwise do so.

As a trooper, you interact with a variety of individuals daily. Although these encounters often involve people from diverse backgrounds with different experiences, most interactions tend to be routine. However, there have been instances that caused a sense of unease in me, prompting heightened vigilance. In some of these situations, the individuals turned out to have active warrants, illegal weapons, or drugs, or likely harbored ill intentions. Had I let my guard down or shown any hesitation, the outcomes might have been drastically different.

In today's fast-paced world, your ability to interpret and respond to subtle cues can be incredibly important across various contexts, from ensuring personal safety to making informed decisions in professional environments such as work. Recognizing when a situation feels off or identifying potential threats quickly can be invaluable.

You need to trust your gut feelings and instincts, as they can serve as powerful assets. Therefore, it's crucial to cultivate and sharpen this natural ability, as it might one day be the key to protecting your life or significantly influencing your achievements.

Additionally, understanding the psychological and biological factors that shape these instincts can provide deeper insights into their reliability and how best to harness them effectively. In Chapter 2, Vigilance: Your First Defense, we discussed that understanding how the brain interprets threats is essential in recognizing why staying alert can be crucial for our safety. We will now build on that knowledge to go over ways to sharpen your awareness and train your "sixth sense."

Understanding Behavior Cues and Body Language

A first step to increasing your ability to recognize potentially dangerous situations is to train yourself to try to recognize nervous behaviors such as fidgeting, rapid blinking, and avoiding eye contact. Of course, these behaviors may not necessarily indicate that you are in danger; they could be related to a medical or psychological condition. However, being able to identify nervous behaviors is crucial for spotting potentially dangerous situations.

The next potential clue to be alert for is signs of aggression. Aggressive body language can manifest in various ways, including tightly closed fists, exaggerated chest expansion, or encroaching on someone's personal space. Recognizing these signs can help in defusing potentially tense situations by addressing the underlying emotions. Additionally, these physical cues often serve as non-verbal communication of dominance or confrontation. By being aware of these gestures, individuals can better navigate social interactions and respond with empathy or assertiveness as needed.

Moreover, understanding the context in which these behaviors occur is crucial, as environmental or situational factors may also play a significant role in influencing such aggressive displays. For instance, in a crowded bar or a packed concert, it's anticipated that people will be in close quarters, and occasional bumps or inadvertent touches are to be expected. In these scenarios, personal space is limited. Conversely, in a shopping mall or a department store, it is unusual for someone to invade your personal space unless they have ulterior motives, such as intimidation or physical harm, or they are mentally unbalanced.

As a former law enforcement officer, I understand that while in uniform, if an individual assumes a fighting stance, it is sufficient grounds to escalate to the next level of force necessary for making an arrest. This posture signals their readiness to use physical force against you. It is not required to wait until they throw a punch, for example. As a civilian, however, your primary responsibility is not to stop aggressive actions and make an arrest; therefore, you might have the opportunity to walk away, depending on the situation. You may choose to strike quickly if the opportunity arises to end the confrontation, particularly if your personal space or boundaries have been breached. This is where having basic self-defense skills is essential. Of course, it is possible that you could be dealing with someone who is mentally unbalanced, and in such cases, walking away might be the best course of action. Ultimately, your response will depend on the specific circumstances at the time.

Paying attention to discrepancies between what people say and how they behave, between verbal and non-verbal cues, can be revealing. These inconsistencies can often signal dishonesty or concealed motives.

When I was a state trooper, this was especially important since some people I encountered would say one thing, but their actions indicated something different. For example, in the late 1990s, I pulled over a vehicle for speeding on a remote highway. The driver, a middle-aged man dressed as a technician, seemed cooperative and assured me he was in a rush to an emergency repair call. His calm demeanor and the way he articulated his words initially diminished my suspicions. However, his furtive glances toward the backseat, perspiration, and the slight tremor in his hands suggested otherwise.

Relying on my academy training, which included noticing actions over words, I decided to conduct a more thorough check. As it turned out, the man's story broke down when a search in plain view revealed a syringe and controlled dangerous substance on the floor of the rear of the vehicle. This incident is similar to what we observe in many politicians: what they say does not necessarily match facts or reality. Similarly, many of us recall how the 2008 financial crisis exposed the discrepancies between what financial institutions claimed about their stability and the risky actions they were taking. These examples underscore the vital lesson that actions often speak louder than words, a truth that remains relevant across various domains of life.

Whether in personal interactions or professional settings, subtle cues like body language, tone of voice, and facial expressions can provide deeper insights into someone's true intentions. Therefore, it's essential to not only listen to words but also observe non-verbal signals to gain a more comprehensive understanding of the underlying message.

It's crucial to be aware of mirroring behaviors because these might indicate someone is attempting to earn your trust for less-than-honest reasons. When someone consistently mimics your actions, speech patterns, or gestures, it might not always be a genuine connection. Instead, it could be a strategic effort to create a sense of rapport and familiarity. Although mirroring can be a natural part of building relationships, it's important to stay vigilant and consider the person's intentions.

In these situations, look for other signs of authenticity and consistency in their behavior over time to get a clearer picture of their true motives. Of course, each situation is different and should be examined in its context. Additionally, trust your instincts and be cautious if you feel something is off. Remember, your intuition can often sense insincerity before your conscious mind does.

Avoiding eye contact, excessive perspiring, or fidgeting are all signs of nervousness or discomfort. Depending on the situation, these observations can be a sign that someone is up to no good.

As a detective specializing in Internet Crimes Against Children, my unit executed numerous search warrants related to child sexual abuse material and other egregious crimes against children. We conducted exhaustive background checks on all individuals known to reside at the targeted premises. Although this meant we typically had a strong preliminary understanding of the likely perpetrator prior to executing the search warrant, it was still imperative to conduct thorough interviews and continue our investigation to substantiate our suspicions.

Usually, the Internet service is registered to a parent, and sometimes, another adult or child in the residence is the perpetrator. As a safety precaution, we have a dedicated entry team trained to enter a residence and secure the occupants prior to the detectives entering. Upon walking into a room full of family members, it is usually obvious who the responsible person is. They are typically perspiring profusely, avoiding eye contact, pale, and, in some cases, visibly shaking. Everyone else is surprised by the intrusion of numerous law enforcement officers inside their home early in the morning, except for the bad guy. They usually have a look indicating they knew it was only a matter of time before they were caught.

This same observation of how everyone in the group is behaving during the execution of a search warrant can be used to evaluate group dynamics to provide crucial warning signals that danger could be on the way. By closely observing the interactions within a group, it becomes possible to identify unusual or tense dynamics or someone behaving differently than the others. These observations can undoubtedly serve as early indicators of a potentially hazardous situation.

Environmental Awareness

One of the most crucial techniques to ensure your safety both in public and at home is maintaining environmental awareness. This involves continuously scanning your surroundings and staying alert to the people and objects around you. You can practice this technique while commuting to work, shopping, or dining out with your family.

For instance, while on your way to dinner with your family, try to look inside the restaurant through a window or glass door before entering, if possible. If there's a violent or disruptive situation occurring, you should avoid entering the venue. Once you determine it's safe and you decide to enter, immediately identify potential escape routes, usually marked with "exit" or "emergency exit" signs. It's essential to know how and where you will escape at any given moment. Your closest exit might be through the kitchen or staff area. In an emergency, don't hesitate to use one of these routes. If you are not near an exit, identify the nearest cover position. Cover, as opposed to concealment, is something that will likely stop a bullet, whereas concealment merely hides you, such as curtains. Choose cover over concealment, if possible. Requesting a seat near an exit is ideal, but it may not always be available. If possible, sit with your back to the wall in a position where you can observe people entering the restaurant or see the room from your seat.

This technique, when paired with scenario training, can be effectively applied in any public setting. The same technique of imagining a crisis while you're waiting in line can be used for sitting in a restaurant with your family. Consider where you would go, what steps you would take, and whether there is cover or concealment available nearby. Actively maintaining awareness of your surroundings and contemplating your actions in the event of certain situations can literally mean the difference between surviving an attack or not.

While it's natural to stay vigilant in high-risk areas like a high-crime section of the city, you may not easily notice changes or reasons to be vigilant in your workplace. Therefore, it's important to be on the lookout for any changes in your work environment, such as unattended bags, out-of-place objects, broken locks, or unfamiliar people, which could indicate a potential problem or danger. By making a conscious effort to be aware of your surroundings daily, you will become accustomed to noticing when something is out of place or "just not right."

Trusting Your Instincts

I'm a firm believer in trusting your instincts or gut feelings. I've often used the elevator scenario when discussing the importance of listening to your gut with others.

In 1984, an American serial killer named Richard Ramirez, also known as the "Night Stalker," terrorized the greater Los Angeles area. His victims ranged across various demographics, and his attacks were characterized by a level of brutality that shocked the nation. He killed many people, but one of the most gripping stories from this horrible period involves a woman named Maria Hernandez, who survived an encounter with Ramirez because she trusted her instincts.

Maria was returning home late at night when she noticed a man lurking near her garage. Despite her initial rationalizations—"It's just a neighbor" or "I'm being paranoid"—her gut screamed danger. When she saw the man approaching, she quickly opened her car door and used it as a shield. The man fired a shot, but the bullet ricocheted off her keys. Maria's quick thinking saved her life as she played dead until Ramirez left the area. Upon entering her home, she found her roommate, Dayle Okazaki, who unfortunately had not survived the encounter with Ramirez. Maria's instinctual response, however, not only saved her own life but provided crucial evidence that eventually led to Ramirez's capture and conviction.

This real-life scenario underscores the importance of trusting your instincts. Just as in the elevator scenario, where one might feel uneasy about stepping in with a stranger, Maria's story illustrates how gut feelings can be a vital survival mechanism. Rationalizing away these feelings can lead to dangerous consequences. Always listen to your body; it is designed to protect you.

It's crucial to consistently hone your situational awareness skills to maintain their sharpness. I've observed that when I'm preoccupied, I sometimes overlook cues or significant changes in my surroundings, only to later think, "Wow, how did I miss that?" This is a common experience for many people. As mentioned earlier, you may find yourself so absorbed or complacent that you can't even recall your drive home from work, for instance. When this occurs, it's important to make a mental note to improve your attentiveness in the future.

Staying Level-Headed

Anxiety can cloud your judgment, making it harder to think straight. Keeping a steady demeanor will help you assess situations more accurately and choose the best course of action. Any situation that has the potential for danger or violence will undoubtedly cause stress and anxiety. An adrenaline surge will affect fine motor skills and your ability to perform simple tasks. Therefore, you need to be thinking about managing everyday stress as well as unexpected stress.

You should develop a strategy for managing stress, such as deep breathing exercises or mindfulness techniques, which can further enhance your ability to stay calm under pressure. There are books and resources available on this subject, such as Dan Millman's *Way of the Peaceful Warrior*, which we discussed in Chapter 2, Vigilance: Your First Defense.

In another main point of his book, Dan learns the importance of staying calm under pressure through his experiences with his mentor, Socrates. A pivotal moment occurs when Dan, initially consumed with anxiety and self-doubt, faces a high-stakes gymnastics competition. Fearing failure, he struggles to maintain his composure. However, thinking about the teachings of Socrates helps him realize that panic and worry only cloud his judgment and hinder his performance. By practicing deep breathing and mindfulness techniques, Dan manages to quiet his mind and approach the competition with a clear and focused mindset. His newly realized calm allows him to perform at his best, illustrating the profound impact of a level-headed approach.

In Chapter 2, Vigilance: Your First Defense, we also mentioned the famous Miracle on the Hudson of 2009, when Captain Chesley "Sully" Sullenberger safely landed US Airways Flight 1549 on the Hudson River after a bird strike disabled the plane's engines. In this situation, his calm demeanor and clear-headed decision-making were crucial. Despite the life-and-death stakes, Sully's ability to remain composed allowed him to think rationally and take decisive action, ultimately saving all 155 passengers aboard. If you haven't listened to the calm radio transmissions during this emergency, it is highly recommended that you do so. Both Dan's and Sully's experiences underscore the importance of maintaining calm in the face of adversity, proving that a steady mind can lead to successful outcomes even in the most challenging situations, including self-defense.

Regular practice develops muscle memory, and when you are confronted with a life-or-death situation, you react to defend yourself. This includes self-defense exercises and other situational awareness skills such as observation and vigilance. Practicing these skills will keep your situational awareness sharp and responsive.

Actively Preparing Is Essential

Foreseeing possible obstacles and planning can ensure you act swiftly and confidently. For example, if you're driving and notice a crowd forming in the street ahead, consider turning around and taking an alternative route. The last thing you want is to drive through a protest that has begun to illegally block the highway. This simple decision to avoid a potential problem can mean the difference between being trapped in your car amidst a blockade of protesters and reaching your destination without issues.

Additionally, adopting the habit of checking your rearview mirror every five to eight seconds, as recommended by many advanced driving instructors, can prevent a rear-end collision. This practice, combined with maintaining adequate spacing between your vehicle and the one in front of you, ensures you have an escape route if needed. Maintaining situational awareness can also help avoid a carjacking, for example, if you notice someone approaching and you have left yourself an out to escape.

Active preparation also involves equipping yourself with the necessary tools at home, in your vehicle, and at work. Having a comprehensive first aid kit, a bleeding control kit, and a basic roadside emergency kit can significantly enhance your safety and preparedness. Ensuring that your vehicle is regularly serviced and in good working condition can help you reach your destination without any problems. For instance, if your car doesn't break down, you're less likely to encounter a criminal looking for their next victim on the highway. Remember, the best way to win a confrontation is to avoid it in the first place. This principle can apply to any situation where you might be at risk. Of course, some scenarios are unavoidable, and no matter what precautions you take, you may still come face to face with a criminal and be compelled to respond or defend yourself. This is where thorough preparation becomes crucial.

Analyze and Grow

After managing any situation, it is crucial to invest time in evaluating your actions and their outcomes to identify areas for growth and development. In Chapter 1, Embarking on Awareness Mastery, we explored the concept of reflecting and learning, which involves considering what transpired during a stressful or unusual situation and deriving lessons from it. If the scenario involved injury or potential danger, analyze what factors could have altered the outcome. Although in some instances, you may have limited alternative options, in many cases, your decisions can significantly influence the result.

For instance, choosing a shortcut to your vehicle that requires walking down a dark or isolated alley poses inherent risks. Similarly, parking your car in a dimly lit area of a parking garage because you are running late for a meeting forces you to traverse that dark area upon your return. If parking in a dimly lit or remote area is unavoidable, consider requesting a security escort and ensure you have self-defense tools like pepper gel or a Taser readily accessible.

Consider another scenario: opting to use an ATM in a secluded area late at night rather than one situated inside a busy convenience store. Many banks have drive-through ATMs installed in older, retrofitted buildings that contain obstructions, creating potential danger zones where criminals can hide, waiting for their next victim. Imagine withdrawing cash and suddenly being confronted by someone pointing a gun at your window, demanding your money. To ensure your safety, it is essential to avoid any drive-through ATMs that have obstructions or limited visibility. Additionally, always be prepared to drive away quickly if you notice any danger or anything that makes you feel uneasy.

My Book Bonuses Page has a link to my YouTube channel for general safety tips. Visit https://mtgsafety.com/ for this and many other great resources.

Now that we have covered the necessary information for you to recognize subtle danger signs, it's time to delve into the basics of concealed carry. Understanding how to responsibly carry and use a concealed handgun is crucial for your safety and the safety of those around you.

Chapter 4

CONCEALED CARRY FUNDAMENTALS

Imagine this: You're out for a late-night walk enjoying the nice weather when, suddenly, you hear footsteps approaching fast from behind. Your heart races, your senses heighten, and your mind races to assess the situation. Are you prepared to defend yourself? This chapter will equip you with the foundational knowledge necessary to confidently carry a concealed handgun, ensuring you're ready for any situation.

In 1984, Bernhard Goetz, a New York City resident, became a controversial figure after he shot four men who he claimed were attempting to rob him on a subway one early afternoon. Mr. Goetz carried a concealed handgun and argued that he acted in self-defense. The incident sparked a national debate over gun control, self-defense laws, and the rights of individuals to protect themselves. Fast forward to recent times, and the debates continue, especially with the rise of incidents where individuals carrying concealed handguns have successfully thwarted potential crimes. In 2020, a man in Texas used his legally carried handgun to stop a shooter in a church, helping to prevent further loss of life.

These instances underscore the importance of being prepared and knowledgeable about self-defense. Although carrying a concealed handgun may not be the right choice for everyone, it is crucial to understand the responsibilities and legal implications involved if you choose to carry. This chapter will provide you with the essential information on proper handling, legal considerations, and practical tips for carrying a concealed handgun, ensuring you are equipped to protect yourself, your family, and others if the need arises.

Since the landmark decision by the U.S. Supreme Court in the *New York State Rifle & Pistol Association v. Bruen (NYSRPA v. Bruen)* case, a significant number of individuals in New Jersey, New York, and other states have applied for and received their carry permits, officially termed in New Jersey as the Permit to Carry a Handgun.

While I firmly believe in the Second Amendment's right to keep and bear arms for self-defense and the protection of one's family, it is crucial to recognize that owning and carrying a loaded firearm in public is not suitable for everyone. The right to own firearms comes with great responsibility. A gun owner is responsible for storing, operating, and maintaining their firearms safely and properly. They must ensure that unauthorized or untrained individuals cannot gain access to their firearms. Additionally, gun owners are responsible for learning and obeying all applicable laws that pertain to the purchase, possession, and use of firearms in their jurisdiction. Firearms themselves are neither inherently safe nor unsafe; for example, an unloaded gun locked in a safe is not dangerous. However, guns are terribly unforgiving of any carelessness or neglect. When gun owners learn and practice responsible gun ownership, guns can be safe.

Many factors should be considered prior to purchasing firearms, but this chapter will focus on concealed carry fundamentals, assuming you either already own firearms or are considering owning them. Some states or jurisdictions have what's called constitutional carry, meaning that if you meet certain requirements, you can carry a loaded handgun under specific conditions and locations. Many states, however, require you to obtain a carry permit, sometimes called a concealed carry permit, which authorizes you to carry a loaded gun in public. It is your responsibility to find out the requirements in your state or jurisdiction prior to carrying a gun. You can usually find this information on your state police website or state attorney general website. You can also inquire with your local police department.

For those considering obtaining a carry permit, I'd like to clarify what a carry permit does not represent. First, a carry permit is not a shield or a protection device. You should avoid conflicts at all costs when carrying, knowing that any physical confrontation will involve at least one gun—yours. Second, a carry permit does not grant you more authority, like a police officer. Possessing a carry permit does not confer any additional rights or powers beyond those of any other citizen who is not carrying a gun. Third, a carry permit is not a means to alter the behavior of others. Brandishing your gun because someone "gets out of line" or says something you don't like will certainly lead to your arrest.

What exactly is a carry permit? A carry permit is an official document that legally authorizes you to carry a firearm. It is vital to understand that this permit allows you to carry a gun, but it does not automatically grant you permission to use it. In fact, individuals who carry firearms are often held to a higher standard of accountability compared with those who do not.

I'm not suggesting that you become a victim, but it is crucial to recognize that carrying a firearm comes with significant responsibility. If you ever find yourself in a situation where you need to use it, law enforcement and prosecutors will closely scrutinize your actions and the circumstances surrounding the incident. They will evaluate who initiated the conflict, whether the situation was escalated and by whom, and what steps you took to avoid using the firearm if possible.

Now, let's discuss some key considerations when deciding if a carry permit is right for you.

Mental and Emotional Preparedness

Can you effectively use your firearm if the need arises? Proper training is essential. If you hesitate during a confrontation, a criminal
might overpower you and use your gun against you. Ensuring that
you are fully prepared and confident in your abilities is crucial.

Legal and Financial Implications

If you discharge your firearm, there is a high likelihood that you will
be arrested, at least initially, for questioning. This does not necessarily mean you will be charged or convicted, but you will need legal
representation. Even if you are cleared, the financial costs can be
significant. Consider the expenses of hiring an attorney and possibly
obtaining liability insurance. And, even if you are not charged criminally, you may have civil action brought against you, which would
require legal representation as well.

Emotional Consequences

Think about the emotional impact of shooting someone. Even in
situations where you had no other choice, the emotional toll can be
profound. This applies not only to you but also to your family. Consider how your spouse or partner feels about you carrying a firearm
and the potential emotional strain it could cause.

Another emotional aspect can relate to beliefs about the ethics
of taking a life, regardless of whether or not it was "justified." When
we talk about ethical responsibility, keep these points in mind:

Your Gun is a Tool of Last Resort: You should only use
your firearm if you feel you are in immediate danger. Ask yourself if
you can use deadly force and if you have the mindset to make that
call, considering both legal and ethical implications. Remember,
"The best way to win a confrontation is to avoid a confrontation."

Understand Local Laws: Some states have "stand your ground" and "castle doctrine" laws. Check with your state on the legality of using force. For instance, in Pennsylvania, the law provides legal protection if someone is breaking into your home, while "stand your ground" laws apply outside your home. However, not all states, such as New Jersey, have these laws in place. In the state of New Jersey, if you can safely retreat in public, you must do so. However, inside your home, you are not obligated to retreat except under certain conditions. New Jersey requires an obvious or perceived threat, not just the mere presence of an outsider in your home.

You should ask yourself, "Am I capable of using deadly force?" Consider whether religious or moral questions or your confidence in your knowledge will impact your ability to respond effectively in a deadly force situation.

Let's consider these elements in more detail. First, you must consider your religious beliefs. Some people believe taking a life is never justified or acceptable, no matter what the circumstances.

Morally, deadly force is a tool of last resort, and if the situation changes, you must adjust the level of force accordingly. For instance, if you are justified in using deadly force and you draw your firearm, but the attacker, upon seeing your gun, drops their gun or other weapon, it is imperative that you de-escalate or reduce the level of force. In this scenario, the immediate deadly threat has ceased, and therefore, you must adapt to the current circumstances by lowering the level of force to match the present justification.

Finally, do you have the legal and ethical knowledge to exercise proper judgment in deciding whether to use deadly force? As mentioned previously, every state or jurisdiction has its laws and restrictions. It is your responsibility to know the laws and circumstances for which deadly force is justified when you are carrying a gun.

Permit Application Process

For those states or jurisdictions requiring a carry permit, you must learn the steps involved in applying for a concealed carry permit, including background checks, fingerprinting, and required training courses. In New Jersey, for example, the process begins online with an electronic application. There are fees, fingerprints, a thorough background check including references that must endorse you, and required training with a qualified firearm instructor. New Jersey has an online training requirement to own or purchase a firearm, even if you don't plan on carrying one for self-defense. Some states have more or fewer requirements, but it is your responsibility to determine what they are.

While firearms are regulated at the federal level, there are significant variations in laws regarding the acquisition, sale, and transportation of firearms depending on your state or locality. For instance, in some states, you are not required to obtain a permit to carry a concealed firearm on your own property or in a business you own. It is your responsibility to understand the specific requirements for obtaining, selling, transferring, carrying, and storing firearms in your state or jurisdiction.

Following the landmark U.S. Supreme Court decision in *NYSRPA v. Bruen*, many states have enacted restrictive gun laws that impose limitations on carry permit holders, including how to obtain a permit, how to carry a firearm, and where it can be carried. These laws have been frequently challenged in the court system, making it crucial to stay informed as the legal landscape is constantly evolving. For example, parts of a relatively new and highly restrictive New Jersey "anti-carry" law have been suspended, but other provisions remain enforceable pending a final court decision.

Understanding the intricacies of these laws is essential because they directly impact where you can legally carry a firearm. Some states, such as New Jersey, prohibit carrying firearms in restaurants or establishments that serve alcohol, even if you are not consuming alcohol yourself. Typically, government establishments, courts, and schools are off-limits as well. It is imperative to be well-versed in the laws and restrictions in the area where you intend to carry a concealed firearm. Stay informed and comply with all applicable regulations to ensure lawful and responsible firearm ownership.

Resources for legal information such as statutes, regulations, and firearm processes in your state can typically be found on state and/or local police agency websites, attorney general websites, and by consulting licensed attorneys who specialize in firearm law in your area.

Responsibilities and Liabilities

Carrying a concealed handgun comes with significant responsibilities. You need to know the legal implications of using your firearm for self-defense. Below is a guide as to what most prosecutors use to determine if deadly force was justified. Of course, local laws will be applicable as the following explanation is a general overview of what law enforcement and prosecutors examine during a use of force incident.

How Most Prosecutors Determine If Deadly Force Was Justified

In most jurisdictions, the use of force is evaluated against the standard of "the reasonable person," which considers what a reasonable individual in the same or similar circumstance would do. Courts have established that prosecutors must not assess the situation with the benefit of hindsight, as hindsight is always considered "20/20." The jury must consider what the individual perceived or experienced during the events that led to the use of deadly force. In other words, try to see what the shooter saw or perceived. It is incumbent upon you to demonstrate that you met the conditions justifying the use of deadly force.

One of the primary factors scrutinized is whether there was an imminent threat or a perceived imminent threat. For example, a neighbor yelling from a second-floor window, "I'm going to kill you," does not constitute an imminent threat. In such a scenario, calling the police to investigate is advisable, but you can safely enter your home or leave the area without immediate danger to your life. Conversely, if you are cornered in an alley and observe your attacker reaching for a gun or knife while advancing toward you, most people would agree that your life is in imminent danger, necessitating immediate action.

The ability, training, and experience of the attacker are also significant factors. For instance, a substantial size mismatch could be crucial. A woman in her 70s weighing 110 pounds should not be expected to physically combat a 6-foot, 5-inch, 250-pound man in his 20s, as he would pose a significant threat to many individuals. On the other hand, if you are highly trained in martial arts and seriously injure or kill your attacker, your use of force may be deemed excessive due to your advanced knowledge and skill in hand-to-hand combat.

In addition, your personal background, training, and experience will be considered as well. Since I have 25 years of law enforcement experience and everything included in such a career in law enforcement, such as 25 years of carrying a gun, extensive firearm training, training and experience in police tactics, and experience in violent confrontations, I would be judged differently than someone with minimal training who has been carrying concealed for two months. Each case is evaluated based on its unique circumstances and the events as they transpired.

Were you minding your own business when attacked, or did you instigate the confrontation? Did you have a safe option to retreat or de-escalate the situation and chose not to do so? This aspect is particularly relevant if your state does not have a "stand your ground" law.

At any point, did the threat decrease or cease, and if so, did you de-escalate or reduce the level of force you were using?

Prosecutors may also examine your public social media accounts to identify any posts or tendencies toward violent behavior. Nothing is off the table for the prosecution. For example, if you "liked" a comment endorsing violence in a video, this could be used against you in a decision to prosecute you for using deadly force. Here's a tragic, real-life example:

In July 2020, Army Sergeant Daniel Perry shot and killed Garrett Foster at a Black Lives Matter protest. This case underscores the complexities of self-defense claims and the influence of intent and premeditation in legal proceedings. Perry, who was convicted of murder for shooting and killing Foster, argued that he acted in self-defense when Foster raised his AK-47 at him. However, prosecutors contended that Perry instigated the shooting, pointing to his past social media posts that seemingly revealed a predisposition toward violence, such as, "I might have to kill a few people on my way to work they are rioting outside my apartment complex," and "I might go to Dallas to shoot looters."

The case also highlights issues within the judicial process. A retired detective revealed that the prosecutor's office did not present exculpatory evidence to the grand jury, which could have impacted the indictment decision. This omission raises questions about fairness and transparency in the legal system. The narrative of this incident parallels the themes in Harper Lee's *To Kill a Mockingbird*, where prejudiced intentions and the suppression of truth significantly influenced the outcome of a trial.

I can't help thinking that if Sergeant Perry had simply turned his car around when he saw the protest forming in the street ahead, the tragic event might have been avoided.

Want to learn more about the use of force?

Check out https://mtgsafety.com/ for my YouTube channel on this subject.

Potential Legal Aftermath of Using Justified Deadly Force

If you are involved in a self-defense shooting incident, here are some things to consider:

- Criminal investigation
  - » Police will investigate, and even if law enforcement determines it was self-defense, the prosecutor can still decide to charge you or present the case to a grand jury to indict you for prosecution.
  - » Fifth Amendment protection against self-incrimination: Remember that prior to answering any questions, you should have an attorney present. While you'll want to tell law enforcement what happened to defend yourself, I would recommend keeping it short and simple, such as, "I want to cooperate but would like an attorney present."
  - » You should expect to at least be brought to the station for questioning. You may be arrested if the police do not have enough evidence or information to determine the aggressor or the victim. You will need an attorney. In some states, you have insurance liability policies available for firearm-related incidents. Some policies provide a group of lawyers you can choose from to call for representation if you are ever in a self-defense situation. I would highly recommend one of these policies if they are available where you live.
- Civil actions: Even if you are not charged criminally, you may have civil actions brought against you by the attacker or the attacker's estate.
- Emotional aftermath: You should know you will experience a psychological effect as well. The following stages of emotion are possible depending on your personality and experience:
  - » Elation: I'm so happy that I survived.

> » Revulsion: I can't stand the thought of violence and/or trauma.
> » Remorse: I feel really bad about what happened.
> » Self-doubt: Was there another way I could have handled this?
> » Acceptance: I had to do it to survive the situation.
> » Post-traumatic stress: You will most likely experience some form of post-traumatic stress and should seek out counseling to help with processing the events and self-reinforcement.

Responsibilities, Safety, and Liabilities

Again, carrying a concealed firearm comes with significant responsibilities. Know the legal implications of using your firearm in self-defense. Start with safety first, however.

To begin with any discussion on concealed carry, we need to learn and always remember the NRA Gun Safety Rules and the Four Basic Rules of Firearm Safety. There are a few variations with some overlap, but for the most part, they exist to ensure we are safe when handling firearms.

The NRA Gun Safety Rules:

- ALWAYS Keep the Gun Pointed in a Safe Direction.
- ALWAYS Keep Your Finger Off the Trigger Until Ready to Shoot.
- ALWAYS Keep the Gun Unloaded Until Ready to Use.

The Four Basic Rules of Firearm Safety:

1. Treat every gun as if it were loaded (All Guns are Always Loaded!).
2. Never point your gun at anything or anyone you're not willing to destroy.

3. Keep your finger off the trigger until sights are on target, and a decision to fire has been made (Golden Rule).
4. Identify (know) your target and what is beyond (and in front of) it.

The Four Basic Rules of Firearm Safety were sanctioned by Lt. Colonel John Dean "Jeff" Cooper, a U.S. Marine deployed during World War II. He also fought in Korea and was an author, a columnist, a professor, and a combat war veteran. He developed modern techniques for combat handgun shooting and founded the American Pistol Institute (API), which became Gunsite Training Center in 1992 and Gunsite Academy in 1999.

Sometimes, people misunderstand the "ready to use" part of the last rule of the NRA Gun Safety Rules. This means any lawful means such as locked in your safe for home protection, lawfully carrying concealed, staged safely around your home, and so on. In other words, your gun is unloaded until you use it, however you plan on using it. It could be training at the range, carrying concealed for protection, or locked in your safe at home.

Some people ask, "Which rules do we follow?" The answer is all of them! There are variations of the gun safety rules, but for the most part, they are all similar in that safety and caution are paramount. If you carry concealed, you will have to unload and load your gun in your car in those instances when you can't carry it with you. During this process, you must be safe and keep your finger off the trigger, for example. You must keep it always pointed in a safe direction. Additionally, if you are in a self-defense situation and are justified in unholstering your gun, these rules are even more important as you will undoubtedly have an adrenaline rush with an associated increased heart rate and breathing rate. Your field of vision will narrow, and your fine motor skills will diminish. At times like this, your muscle memory and practiced skills will be important in keeping others around you who are not involved in the attack safe from an "accidental"—or more accurately, negligent—discharge.

You should know that you are responsible for every bullet that exits your gun. If you miss your target and hit an innocent person behind the bad guy you're aiming for, you are responsible!

And never use drugs or alcohol while carrying a personal protection firearm. If you are ever involved in a shooting, you may be tested for drug or alcohol use.

Choosing the Right Firearm

When selecting a firearm for home defense, there are many factors to consider. Similarly, choosing a firearm for concealed carry also requires careful consideration of various elements. In this section, we will delve into the important aspects you should consider, in addition to the points previously discussed regarding selecting a firearm for home defense.

Firearm Features to Consider

When selecting a firearm for concealed carry, it is crucial to consider three main categories: (1) size and caliber, (2) comfort and concealability, and (3) reliability and maintenance. In addition, there are pros and cons to choosing a semi-automatic versus a revolver.

For instance, semi-automatics typically have a higher capacity compared to revolvers of similar size. However, revolvers are known for their exceptional reliability and infrequent malfunctions. And although revolvers are usually bulkier and heavier than semi-automatics of a similar size, they offer a distinct advantage in certain close combat situations.

Consider a scenario where you must press the muzzle of your firearm against an attacker due to a close attack encounter. With a semi-automatic, if the upper slide is moved even slightly during this confrontation, it can cause a condition known as *out of battery*, rendering the gun unable to fire because it is not in the proper configuration.

On the other hand, a revolver will still fire when the muzzle is pressed up against an attacker.

Achieving the right balance between size, weight, and stopping power is essential. For instance, smaller caliber firearms may be easier to carry and conceal, but they often lack the necessary stopping power and can be more challenging to handle for individuals with larger hands compared to guns with a larger frame and caliber.

Comfort is also very important. Your concealed carry firearm must be as comfortable as possible and easy to conceal. Factors to consider include grip size, holster compatibility, and necessary clothing adjustments. Your wardrobe plays a significant role, as carrying a firearm in dress clothing differs from carrying it in casual attire like shorts and a polo shirt. Additionally, your body type may affect how well certain firearms fit and can be concealed.

You can't forget about maintenance and reliability, as they are paramount. Select a reputable brand known for reliability and ease of maintenance. Regular cleaning and upkeep are necessary to ensure your firearm functions properly when needed.

Choosing a firearm that is too large or heavy, or one that is difficult to conceal, will likely result in you opting not to carry it. Consequently, you may leave it at home, rendering it useless in a self-defense scenario. On the other hand, if your firearm is too small, you might face challenges operating it, particularly during a reload or in the event of a malfunction, where precise handling is crucial.

I recommend finding an instructor who has many different types, sizes, and calibers of handguns for you to try out. You can also visit a shooting range with an associated gun shop because they typically will rent guns. It could be a good idea to try out as many different guns as you can in order to evaluate the different aspects and get a feel for which ones you prefer.

When it comes to accessories and aftermarket parts for concealed carry guns, I have a personal preference to avoid altering the original configuration of my firearm. I prefer to keep my concealed carry gun mostly as it comes from the manufacturer. Adding accessories, such as lights or optics, can lead to complications. I've observed instances at the range where these additions get caught on clothing when people attempt to draw their guns. Extra accessories also contribute to increased bulkiness.

Although I do believe that having a light is beneficial, I recommend carrying a flashlight separately rather than attaching it to your gun. A small handheld flashlight can be a practical solution for concealed carry individuals. Regarding optics, I have no issues with red dots or other types; however, they come with their own set of potential problems, such as battery failure. My primary concern with these accessories is their tendency to snag on clothing, which can be problematic in a self-defense situation.

I advocate for a minimalist approach, favoring a basic gun with iron sights. Most confrontations happen at close range, typically within 3 to 5 yards, and unfold very quickly. Statistically, this is the most common scenario you might face when you need to use your firearm. Keeping this in mind, opting for a straightforward setup can be more practical and reliable.

Transitioning now to key principles of effective concealment, here are some things to keep in mind when choosing a firearm:

- **Flatness and Concealability:** This is the most crucial factor affecting both concealment and comfort. Generally, the thinner and shorter the pistol, the more comfortable it is to carry. However, proficiency in using the firearm is essential, and if you have larger hands, a smaller gun may be challenging to shoot and manipulate properly. In addition, the holster must be suitable for concealed carry. An observant individual should not suspect you are carrying a firearm.

- **Power:** Consider the caliber. A minimum of 9 mm or 0.38 Special is highly recommended. Sometimes, compromises are necessary to balance comfort and firepower.
- **Accessibility:** Immediate access to your firearm is a must since many deadly force situations occur very fast at close range:
  - » **Retention:** Your holster should securely retain your pistol to your body. You need to train for weapon retention!
  - » **Comfort:** The holster must be comfortable. If it's not, you will eventually stop carrying it, and if your gun is left at home or locked away because it's uncomfortable, it won't be of any use. You can get a variety of holsters and see which one works for you.

You should also do the following if you plan to carry concealed:

1. **Choose Appropriate Clothing:** Wear attire that effectively conceals your firearm without drawing attention to it. Select patterns and fabrics that obscure any outlines. *Printing*, or the ability to see your gun under clothing, while not necessarily illegal for concealed carry, will give away the fact that you are carrying a gun, removing the element of surprise necessary to maintain a strategic advantage.
2. **Select the Right Holster:** Invest in a quality holster that ensures your gun stays hidden, secure, and easily accessible when needed (I will talk more about this next).
3. **Mind Your Movements:** Be conscious of how you move, sit, and bend to prevent accidental exposure of your concealed carry.
4. **Regular Practice:** Consistently practicing drawing from concealment is crucial for developing muscle memory and decreasing response time during critical situations. To ensure the effectiveness of your training, wear the same clothing and gear to the shooting range that you use in your daily life. This

will allow you to safely practice drawing in the exact clothes and holster configuration you wear when out in public.

Equally important are the fundamental principles of concealment. These principles include choosing appropriate attire that effectively hides your firearm, ensuring the holster retains your weapon securely, and maintaining a low profile to avoid drawing unnecessary attention. By integrating these principles with regular practice, you enhance your ability to respond efficiently and discreetly in real-world scenarios.

By adhering to these principles, you enhance your ability to stay prepared and protect yourself while keeping your tactical advantage intact.

Proper Equipment

Now, I'll go over some of the more essential items to consider when carrying concealed. Be aware that although this list is thorough, it doesn't cover every single thing you might need to consider.

Holsters

As we've talked about, selecting the right firearm is crucial—but it is equally important to choose the proper equipment, such as the right holster and ammunition. It's worth noting that some states have defined "holster" by statute. For instance, in New Jersey, a "holster" is defined as "a device or sheath that securely retains a handgun which, at a minimum, conceals and protects the main body of the firearm, maintains the firearm in a consistent and accessible position, and renders the trigger covered and inaccessible while the handgun is fully seated in the holster."

Not all states regulate holsters, so it's essential to check with your state or jurisdiction to determine if there are specific requirements you must meet. Ensuring compliance can help you avoid legal complications and ensure your safety.

There are many types of holsters available, but at the very least, a holster should properly secure your gun to your body and cover the trigger area. This is crucial to prevent objects like keys or jacket pull-strings from entering the trigger area and causing a negligent discharge. I recommend a Kydex-type holster, which is form-fitted to your gun for a secure fit. There are hybrid holsters that are made of a combination of form-fitting Kydex specific for your make and model for retention and leather portions for comfort. Additionally, holsters come with different levels of retention, meaning you may need to depress or move a lever to release the gun. The more actions required to release the gun, the higher the level of retention. For example, uniformed law enforcement officers typically use Level 3 retention holsters because their guns are usually exposed in full view. They also train extensively with these holsters to ensure they can quickly and efficiently draw their weapons when needed. You should follow suit and practice with the holster you use when you conceal carry to ensure you can respond effectively in any situation.

As with selecting the proper firearm, I would recommend finding a qualified firearm instructor who should have multiple holsters available for you to examine and select from.

Finally, if you are going to carry a concealed firearm inside a waist pack or handbag designed for concealed carry, it should be in a proper holster inside the bag. Be sure to check with your state or jurisdiction as many places have laws regarding how you can carry your gun. For example, in New Jersey, your loaded gun must be "under your immediate control" at all times. Handbags or waist packs are not prohibited by statute; however, they are gray areas since once you remove the bag from your body, it is not "under your immediate control" necessarily. I recommend if you are going to use one of these bags or packs, it must be secured to your body, and if you remove it for any reason, you must unload and properly secure your firearm.

Ammunition

There are numerous types of commercial ammunition available on the market. It's essential to check with your state or local jurisdiction to determine if there are any restrictions on the type of ammunition you can carry. For instance, in New Jersey, current law restricts hollow point ammunition to active-duty law enforcement personnel only. Thanks to a recent federal court decision, there is an exception for certain qualified retired law enforcement officers as defined under the Law Enforcement Officers Safety Act (LEOSA). However, New Jersey law has not yet been updated to reflect this recent decision.

The law restricting hollow point ammunition may seem counterintuitive because hollow point rounds are generally considered safer for self-defense. These rounds expand upon impact, reducing the risk of over-penetration. Over-penetration is undesirable in defensive shooting because it increases the risk of the bullet traveling through the attacker and potentially harming an unintended target.

Hollow point ammunition is legal to own in New Jersey: you can use it for home defense, shoot it at the range, and purchase it. However, you cannot carry it in your concealed carry gun unless you are an active-duty law enforcement officer or a qualified retired law enforcement officer carrying under LEOSA.

An excellent alternative to hollow point ammunition is Hornady Critical Duty or Critical Defense. These rounds feature a polymer-filled hollow tip, making them legal to carry in New Jersey. Studies have shown that they behave similarly to traditional hollow point ammunition, but since the tip is filled with polymer, New Jersey does not classify them as hollow point rounds.

Finally, it is crucial to use the appropriate ammunition for your concealed carry firearm. Certain high-powered loads, such as +P+, can potentially lead to structural damage to your gun.

It's advisable to test various types of ammunition at the range to evaluate how your firearm performs. This hands-on experience, combined with recommendations specific to your needs, will guide you in making an informed decision about the best ammunition for your purposes.

See this video I created on selecting an Everyday Carry Gun on the Book Bonuses Page: https://mtgsafety.com

First Aid/Bleeding Control Kit

As a former paramedic, I strongly recommend that everyone always have a well-equipped first aid kit and a bleeding control kit readily accessible—whether at home, in your vehicle, at work, or the shooting range.

There are various types and sizes of these kits available. In fact, you can find compact versions that are small enough to fit in your car, purse, or even your range bag for training purposes.

Bleeding control kits are particularly crucial as they typically contain a tourniquet, hemostatic dressings, and other essential items designed to manage life-threatening bleeding effectively.

In situations where you might need to use your firearm for self-defense, having a bleeding control kit on hand could be vital for treating yourself or others.

You should take a course to become certified in CPR/AED, First Aid, and Bleeding Control. Short videos are even available online to learn how to apply a tourniquet to yourself in an emergency.

I have a special video dedicated to this topic. See the Book Bonuses Page for the link: https://mtgsafety.com/

Flashlight

If you carry concealed, you should always carry a flashlight. It doesn't have to be large, and many newer flashlights have strobe functions. Flashlights can be a great non-lethal form of self-defense. For example, when walking to your vehicle, if someone is approaching, you can shine the strobe light into their face while turning and running away or reaching for your concealed carry gun or pepper gel. In addition, having a flashlight can help if you find yourself walking in a dimly lit area or need to check your firearm under low-light conditions, such as when unloading or loading.

Training to Boost Confidence and Dry-Fire Devices

I always emphasize the critical importance of training. Nothing matches the experience of live-fire training at the range. It's advisable to periodically engage a qualified instructor to evaluate your technique and provide additional training and recommendations.

Many individuals harbor doubts or safety concerns when carrying concealed for the first time. From my experience, there are two effective ways to overcome this. Firstly, train regularly with your firearm to become more comfortable with its handling and shooting. Secondly, carry your firearm as often as possible to make it a natural part of your routine. The more you do it, the more accustomed you will become.

But what happens when you can't make it to the range for training? Various factors like work, home life, expenses, and weather conditions can sometimes prevent you from visiting the range. In such cases, having an alternative training method is essential. One effective alternative is dry-fire training.

Dry-fire training involves using your actual gun or a training device to practice fundamental firearm skills. Numerous dry-fire devices and equipment are available to facilitate this, such as the SIRT, Mantis X10 Elite, and Umarex. For example, Umarex air guns offer a blowback feature that simulates the recoil of firing a real gun. These devices come in various gun models and calibers. A Glock 19 training device, for instance, looks and feels like an actual Glock 19. Additionally, you can purchase an optional laser barrel to replace and use a laser function for evaluating your shooting technique.

These training devices allow you to consistently practice your fundamental techniques in the comfort of your own home. Advanced devices like the Mantis X10 Elite can sync with an app on your cell phone, providing a wealth of data to evaluate your shooting technique. This app can even identify issues and offer recommendations to correct them. The Mantis device can also be used for live-fire training at the range.

Safes and Proper Storage

When not carrying your firearm, it is crucial to have a reliable method for securing it, whether at home, in your vehicle, or at work. There will be situations where you cannot or do not want to carry your firearm, necessitating proper storage. Typically, this means keeping the firearm unloaded with ammunition stored separately. Be diligent and always know that "your gun is always somewhere."

For vehicle security, many portable safes are available that can be anchored to your seat frame or another fixed structure within your car. Additionally, some manufacturers produce custom vaults designed specifically for center consoles or other areas of your vehicle, offering enhanced security and convenience.

At home, having a safe is essential since you won't always have your firearm on your person. There are a wide variety of home safes and storage devices to choose from, including large and small safes, trigger locks, key locks, and electronic biometric options. You need to consider balancing safety and accessibility. The more secure your firearm is, the longer it will take to access it during an emergency. Conversely, quicker access solutions can pose risks, such as unauthorized access by children. Not only is it a crime in many states to leave a loaded firearm accessible to minors, but as a responsible gun owner, you must keep your guns properly secured from people who shouldn't have access to them.

I personally don't use biometric or electronic safes for my vehicle as extreme weather conditions can affect their performance. I think they're fine for home or office, but I typically use a key lock for my vehicle to ensure it will open. Some biometric or electronic safes do have key backups as well.

Make sure to visit https://mtgsafety.com/ for recommended book bonuses and products discussed in the book.

Using a Public Restroom when Carrying Concealed

I've been asked about this in the past, and it is indeed a safety concern. When you need to use a public restroom, there are a few important considerations to keep in mind.

First, if possible, if in a men's room, opt for a stall where you can close the door, providing you with more privacy and security. This is generally the safest option.

If a stall is not available and you must use a urinal, I recommend selecting one that is away from others, ideally close to a wall or a privacy panel. This will help minimize your exposure and increase your sense of security.

Second, be aware of anyone walking in your vicinity. If someone walks by, turn your head from side to side as they pass. This will give you a wider area of peripheral vision to ensure they are just walking by and not getting closer to you. It will also let them know you are aware of them.

Third, ensure that your concealed carry handgun is securely fastened so it won't fall or drop from your belt or clothing when unzipping or unbuckling your belt. You need to hold your gun and holster in place while using the urinal. In most cases, depending on your body type, holster, and its position, you can do this with your arm or elbow area.

When using a restroom stall (women's or men's restroom) and having sit down, it is advisable to remove your concealed carry gun from your body while it remains in its holster. Do not take your gun out of the holster!

After detaching your gun/holster from your belt or clothing, hold it securely between your legs, ensuring the firearm is pointed in a safe direction. Avoid placing your gun and belt on the coat hook because this makes it easy for someone to reach over and steal it. Additionally, refrain from setting your firearm on any table, shelf, or toilet paper dispenser. Keeping it between your legs, still within the holster and pointed in a safe direction, allows you to always maintain immediate control and ensures readiness in case of an attack in the stall.

Although this method requires some practice, it can be performed safely. Removing your gun from its holster is unsafe in that environment, and placing it on any surface risks it being knocked off or forgotten in the stall.

If you carry your gun in a handbag or waist pack designed for concealed carry, be sure to place the bag or pack between your legs and not on the floor or hanging from the coat hook.

Effective Training and Practice

Even if you are a long-time firearm owner or shooter, before carrying concealed, you should have basic firearm skills mastered, including the safe practice of drawing from a holster. By "mastered," I mean, you should be entirely comfortable handling your firearm and performing essential manipulations such as safely drawing from a holster, loading, unloading, reloading, and clearing any malfunctions. These actions should be so ingrained that they become second nature.

In a self-defense situation where you might need to use deadly force, you will need to rely on these fundamentals. Your heart rate will be elevated, and adrenaline will surge. In such high-stress moments, having these skills deeply embedded in your muscle memory can make all the difference.

Basic Firearm Skills: Enlist the expertise of a certified firearm instructor to effectively learn the essential techniques of shooting, such as proper grip, stance, sight alignment, sight picture, and trigger discipline. These foundational skills are critical and will be your go-to methods during high-pressure scenarios, like self-defense situations. Additionally, consider incorporating regular practice sessions and stress-inoculation training to better prepare yourself for real-life confrontations. Remember, consistency and repetition in training are key to building muscle memory, which can significantly enhance your performance under stress.

Drawing and Reholstering: Practice drawing your firearm from concealment and reholstering it safely. Speed and precision are crucial in high-stress situations. However, finding a range where you can practice drawing from a holster can be challenging because many individuals lack the proper technique, posing safety risks to everyone nearby. To address this, you should seek out a qualified firearm instructor who can guide you through the steps necessary to safely practice and master this technique.

Scenario-Based Training: Immerse yourself in training that replicates real-life self-defense scenarios. Such training is crucial for honing your ability to make quick decisions and execute effective responses under pressure. This concept has been emphasized in earlier chapters as an essential component for developing the knowledge and skills necessary to make informed decisions regarding the use of deadly force.

During high-stress, high-adrenaline incidents, individuals have reported experiencing a loss of fine motor skills, tunnel vision, and temporary memory loss. One effective strategy to mitigate these effects is to heed the advice of U.S. Army General George Patton, who famously stated, "Train like you fight and fight like you train." This guidance underscores the importance of practicing in environments that closely replicate actual combat conditions.

Although it's impossible to recreate or anticipate every scenario you might encounter, adopting a defensive mindset in your training can significantly improve your readiness. We will delve into this approach in more detail soon.

Drawing from General Patton's wisdom, we can infer that individuals typically fight in the manner they have been trained. This principle holds significant importance, particularly when considering how you conduct your training at the range. It is crucial to recognize that in a real-life scenario, your reactions will likely mirror those practiced during training. However, it is essential to account for the heightened stress levels you will experience in such situations. Therefore, it is imperative that you make every moment of your training count and prepare as thoroughly as possible.

I've conducted numerous scenario-based exercises with students, often posing the question: "What would you do?" The diversity of answers is astonishing, reflecting everyone's different experiences and training backgrounds. Additionally, discussing real-life incidents, analyzing the responses, and contemplating whether you would have acted similarly can provide valuable insights.

While it's impossible to predict every potential situation or event, we can train and leverage that knowledge and experience to make sound decisions when the time comes.

Now that you have a solid understanding of the fundamentals of concealed carry, it's time to delve deeper into developing the mindset necessary to effectively use your skills in real-world situations. In the next chapter, Crafting a Defensive Mindset, we will explore how to cultivate situational awareness, mental preparedness, and defensive techniques to stay ahead of potential threats.

Chapter 5

CRAFTING A DEFENSIVE MINDSET

It is often said that "the best defense is a good offense," but in the realm of personal safety, a well-crafted defensive mindset is the true key to mastering situational awareness and concealed carry.

What Is a Defensive Mindset?

A defensive mindset is a mental framework that prioritizes safety, situational awareness, and proactive measures to prevent and respond to threats. It enhances personal security, reduces the likelihood of becoming a victim, and enhances the ability to react swiftly and effectively during crises.

On April 15, 2013, the Boston Marathon was abruptly disrupted by two bombs that exploded near the finish line, resulting in several deaths and hundreds of injuries. Surrounded by chaos, the quick actions of bystanders and first responders exemplified the essence of a defensive mindset. Carlos Arredondo, a spectator and volunteer, immediately sprang into action. Despite the risk to his own safety, he used his belt as a tourniquet to help save the life of a gravely injured victim. His situational awareness and ability to react swiftly and effectively exemplified the importance of a defensive mindset in such crises.

Developing Situational Awareness

In Chapters 1 and 2, we discussed situational awareness as being aware of your surroundings at any given moment in public spaces as well as at home. We also stressed the importance of vigilance, the ability to maintain attention and focus on potential threats in your environment. Both involve preparedness. There are many methods of learning how to be aware and pay attention to details in your environment.

To help you start developing these skills, we covered the importance of honing your observation skills to effectively scan your surroundings, spot potential dangers, and detect unusual activities. This is an essential part of developing situational awareness. Enhancing these abilities involves not just seeing but truly noticing details. It's about training your mind to pick up on subtle cues and patterns that others may overlook. This skill is invaluable in various scenarios, from personal safety to professional environments.

Furthermore, situational awareness is not just about external observation but also about understanding your own responses and biases. Recognizing how stress or preconceived notions can affect your perception is crucial. By doing so, you can ensure a more accurate and comprehensive assessment of your environment.

Constantly scrutinizing your environment and responding to routine behaviors can foster feelings of anxiety and paranoia. It's essential to practice mindfulness and develop a habit of being aware of your surroundings without becoming overly suspicious. Striking a balance between vigilance and a sense of normalcy is key. Embracing mindfulness techniques, such as deep breathing and grounding exercises, can help maintain this equilibrium. Additionally, recognizing that most daily interactions are benign and harmless can further ease unnecessary stress. By cultivating a mindful and balanced approach, you can stay aware without compromising your peace of mind.

Participating in practical exercises like drills and simulations is crucial for improving your capacity to stay alert and react effectively in stressful situations. These activities help build muscle memory, enhance decision-making skills, and foster a calm demeanor under pressure. Additionally, regularly practicing such scenarios can uncover potential weaknesses in your response strategies, allowing you to address them proactively. Remember, the more realistic and varied the simulations, the better prepared you'll be for actual emergencies. Consistent training not only boosts individual performance but also strengthens team coordination and communication, ensuring a cohesive and efficient response when it matters most.

Building Mental Resilience

There are many techniques for managing adrenaline and maintaining composure during high-pressure situations. Dealing with stress effectively involves mastering methods to control adrenaline and remain calm while under pressure. Here are some strategies to help you manage and reduce stress:

1. **Deep Breathing Exercises:** Practicing deep breathing can help regulate your heart rate and calm your mind. Try inhaling deeply through your nose, holding it for a few seconds, and then exhaling slowly through your mouth. You can use this technique any time of the day or night.
2. **Mindfulness and Meditation:** Engage in mindfulness practices or meditation to stay grounded and focused. This can help clear your mind and reduce the impact of stressors. Take some time alone to practice mindfulness and meditation.

3. **Physical Activity:** Regular exercise can be an excellent way to manage stress. Physical activity helps release endorphins, which can improve your mood and reduce anxiety. Get into an exercise routine. If you prefer outdoor activities, have some equipment inside, such as a treadmill or stationary bike, to use during inclement weather.

4. **Time Management:** Organize your tasks and prioritize them to avoid feeling overwhelmed. Break down large projects into manageable steps and tackle them one at a time. You'd be surprised how much organizing according to priority helps reduce stress.

5. **Positive Visualization:** Visualize positive outcomes and success in your endeavors. This can boost your confidence and help you approach challenges with a positive mindset. You should do this with imaginary scenarios for self-defense as discussed earlier, as well as real-life activities you have planned.

6. **Progressive Muscle Relaxation:** This technique involves tensing and then slowly relaxing each muscle group in your body. It can help reduce physical tension and promote relaxation. You can combine this activity with mindfulness and meditation.

7. **Support System:** Reach out to friends, family, or colleagues for support. Talking about your stressors with someone you trust can provide relief and offer new perspectives.

8. **Adequate Rest:** Ensure you are getting enough sleep. Lack of rest can exacerbate stress and make it more difficult to manage. Aim for 7–9 hours of quality sleep each night. Many people do not get enough sleep!

9. **Healthy Diet:** Maintain a balanced diet to keep your energy levels stable. Avoid excessive caffeine and sugar, which can lead to energy crashes and increased stress. You can improve your diet and quickly see the results.

10. **Professional Help:** If stress becomes overwhelming, consider seeking help from a mental health professional. Therapy or counseling can provide you with strategies tailored to your specific needs. Don't wait until you feel overwhelmed or a situation feels out of control to seek help.

By incorporating these techniques into your routine, you can better manage adrenaline and maintain composure during high-pressure situations. Remember, it's important to find what works best for you and make self-care a priority.

Decision-Making Strategies

When confronted with potential hazards or urgent situations, making swift and well-informed decisions is crucial. The following strategies can help enhance your ability to act decisively and effectively under pressure:

1. **Stay Calm:** Maintaining composure allows you to think clearly and avoid panic, which can cloud judgment. Practice deep breathing or mindfulness techniques to help you stay centered. Don't let your emotions control your reaction or behavior.
2. **Gather Information Quickly:** Assess the situation by gathering as much relevant information as possible in a short amount of time. Identify the nature of the threat, potential consequences, and available resources.
3. **Prioritize:** Determine which actions are most critical and address them first. Use the triage approach to quickly evaluate what needs immediate attention and what can be deferred. First responders are trained to do this when responding to mass casualty incidents.

4. **Rely on Training:** If you have received any emergency response training, rely on those protocols. Familiarity with standard procedures can streamline decision-making and reduce hesitation. Try and get additional training when available.

5. **Communicate Clearly:** Ensure that all involved parties understand the situation and the actions being taken. Clear and concise communication can prevent misunderstandings and coordinate efforts more effectively.

6. **Use the 10-10-10 Rule:** Consider the impact of your decision in 10 minutes, 10 months, and 10 years. This perspective helps balance short-term urgency with long-term consequences.

7. **Trust Your Instincts:** In high-pressure situations, your intuition can be a valuable guide. Often, gut feelings are based on subconscious recognition of patterns or previous experiences. Rely on your "sixth sense."

8. **Learn from Experience:** Once the emergency has subsided, it is crucial to take the time to reflect on the events that transpired, the decisions that were made, and the outcomes of those decisions. Engaging in this thoughtful review can significantly enhance your ability to manage future crises more effectively. This reflective practice is an excellent way to continually learn and improve.

By incorporating these strategies, you can enhance your decision-making skills and better navigate emergencies with confidence and clarity.

There are organizations that offer specialized training to foster mental toughness, a crucial attribute for handling stress and adversity effectively. These programs often include techniques such as mindfulness, cognitive behavioral strategies, and stress management exercises. Additionally, defensive readiness can be bolstered through practical drills, self-defense courses, and scenario-based training that prepares individuals for real-life challenges.

I highly recommend researching and selecting a solid self-defense training academy with a history of good reviews for learning and maintaining techniques you can use to protect yourself and your loved ones. Once you select a training school, make the commitment to attend regularly.

Incorporating mindfulness practices, such as meditation and deep breathing exercises, can further bolster one's ability to maintain mental clarity under pressure.

The Defensive Shooter Mindset

If you are ever in a deadly force situation or confrontation you cannot avoid, and you've made the decision you must use your gun for self-defense, you should have a *defensive shooter mindset.*

When discussing self-defense, it is crucial to consider what is often termed "defensive accuracy." In a defensive mindset, the focus shifts from the precise accuracy required at a shooting range to a balance between speed and accuracy. While honing your skills to achieve a tight, centered shot group is beneficial for evaluation and skill development, during self-defense situations, aiming for the center of mass—typically the largest part of a person or target—is more practical.

This technique, sometimes referred to as point shooting, emphasizes aiming at center mass while balancing speed with accuracy. Utilizing the front sight only can further enhance speed. In critical moments, the ability to quickly come on target and pull the trigger can be the determining factor between walking away safely and not surviving the encounter.

Sight Alignment and Sight Picture

Proper sight alignment involves accurately lining up the front and rear sights of your firearm. Sight picture, on the other hand, is the process of positioning these properly aligned sights onto your target.

The key to both is focusing on the front sight for accurate placement, ideally while aiming with both eyes open to maintain depth perception and a wider field of peripheral vision. This technique is crucial in threat environments, where situational awareness of your surroundings is imperative. During range training, this process is typically performed methodically to ensure precision, as the more accurately the sights are aligned with the target, the more precise the shots will be.

However, in defensive shooting scenarios, time is a critical factor because most life-threatening encounters happen very quickly and typically at close distances of about 3–5 yards. In such situations, aiming at center mass becomes essential, and this is where the concept of a flash-sight picture comes into play. Instead of taking time to achieve a perfect sight picture as you would in a controlled environment, a flash sight picture allows for quick target acquisition and rapid engagement. In these high-stress moments, your sight alignment may not be perfect since there isn't time to meticulously line up the front and rear sights. Nevertheless, even with slightly imperfect alignment, aiming for center mass increases the likelihood of hitting your target effectively and reaching your goal, which is to stop the action.

This defensive shooting technique can be used for public or home self-defense situations.

Additional Fundamentals

Other fundamentals to consider include *breath control, trigger control, follow-through,* and *grip.*

Breath Control involves managing your breathing while shooting to ensure it doesn't affect your accuracy. Typically, this is done consciously at the range. However, in a high-stress situation, you'll need to rely on how you trained because your attention will have other priorities. One effective method is to inhale, exhale halfway, and hold your breath to take the shot. Keeping some air in your lungs helps maintain your natural aiming area or point. You should breathe normally when you're not squeezing the trigger and avoid holding your breath too long as this can lead to over-staring, shaking, or flinching. In sudden attack incidents, you might not have time to focus on breathing, but it remains a fundamental aspect of accurate shooting.

Trigger Control or manipulation, involves the placement of your finger on the trigger and the motion of squeezing. Place the middle of the first section of your index finger solidly on the trigger's face. It's crucial to squeeze rather than *pull* to ensure a consistent front-to-back motion, which helps keep the gun steady. A highly effective way to practice this is through dry-fire exercises, as discussed in Chapter 4, Concealed Carry Fundamentals."

Follow-Through ensures the gun is ready to fire another shot. This is achieved by holding the trigger to the rear after squeezing and taking your shot, allowing you to manage recoil. You'll momentarily come off target due to recoil, but you should quickly re-establish your sight picture by focusing on the front sight. Then, release the trigger only to the reset point or click as you prepare for your next shot. This technique maintains focus on the front sight and reinforces trigger control for multiple shots.

Grip is crucial and should be established before incorporating the other fundamentals. A proper grip helps manage recoil, prevent malfunctions, and operate the gun efficiently for shooting, reloading, and other tasks. The firing hand should apply pressure like a firm handshake while the support hand clamps down like a vise. For semi-automatic firearms, ensure your hand is as high on the grip as possible under the backstrap. Wrap your middle, ring, and pinky fingers around the grip, keeping them side-by-side, with the middle finger just below the trigger guard. Keep your index finger straight along the gun frame, outside the trigger guard, until you're ready to shoot.

Training to perfect these fundamentals will engrain these techniques so that you perform them instinctively, especially in high-stress situations. This muscle memory is what you'll rely on during a self-defense incident.

Elements of Good Shooting Position/Defensive Shooting Skills

Although there is no substitute for a comprehensive defensive shooting course, the following are some essential elements that should be included in a typical defensive shooting course:

Consistency: You must be consistent when you train. Consistency will allow you to hone your skills while developing muscle memory. Remember, muscle memory is key to improving your shooting consistency. In addition, you are most likely to react with muscle memory in a high-stress situation. Remember, as the saying goes, when you train to fight, you fight as you train.

Balance: Balancing your stance and overall shooting platform is always important and will be beneficial when responding to recoil. If you need to fire multiple shots, you will have to "reset" after each shot, meaning recoil reaction and target re-acquisition. Having a balanced shooting platform is essential for this to occur proficiently.

Support: Providing proper support will ensure the most stable shooting platform. Natural aiming area (NAA), also referred to as natural point of aim, is the natural position of the gun's sights when a shooter is relaxed in their shooting position. It minimizes the effects of body movement on the firearm's impact point and allows you to make shots with both accuracy and precision. You are using your non-muscular support to provide the shooting platform. This helps with multiple shots and eliminates muscle fatigue and shaking associated with muscle tension.

Stance: Here are some things to keep in mind about your stance:

- Various shooting stances can be effectively taught by a certified instructor in either a classroom setting or at a shooting range. Some stances include the two-handed standing-ready position, low ready, and retention ready/high ready stances. Additionally, the isosceles, Weaver, and kneeling positions, as

well as their respective variations, are also fundamental techniques. Each of these positions offers distinct advantages in
different shooting scenarios, emphasizing the importance of
mastering a range of stances to enhance both accuracy and
safety.

- Engaging with a qualified instructor ensures that you learn
proper form and technique, which is crucial for effective and
responsible firearm handling. For example, if you are standing straight up as opposed to slightly leaning forward, your
recoil management will not be as effective. You may not even
realize you're doing this, but a qualified firearm instructor
will immediately notice and correct your position.

- As you practice different stances and variations at the range,
you will develop one that is most comfortable for you, which
you will most likely use in a self-defense situation.

As a state trooper, I used a modified Weaver stance, more like a
fighting stance. This shooting position kept my body slightly bladed,
ensuring that my strong side or firearm was away from the person
I was interacting with. We were always taught to keep our exposed
firearms away from people as much as possible. Hence, my stance
was always a modified Weaver stance when talking to people, and it
was also an advantageous position if I needed to fight. My feet were
spread, my strong side was slightly back from my weak side, and I
was balanced to react effectively if I got struck or pushed.

The Weaver stance, although effective in certain shooting scenarios, is not always recommended for police officers. This is because
the bladed body position leaves the front or forward-bladed area
exposed, without the protective coverage of body armor. Therefore,
it is generally advised that officers maintain a more squared stance
when shooting to ensure the full protection of their body armor. Despite this, my training emphasized maintaining a bladed stance with
my firearm positioned away from the person I was interacting with.

There are some disadvantages to the Weaver position. It is challenging to keep your gun on target if you must move, which is likely to happen in a firefight situation. However, the Weaver stance allows for a push-pull technique to solidify your shooting platform even more. Modifying the Weaver into a fighting stance was more beneficial to me than standing straight in an isosceles position, which is not ideal when interacting with someone. However, if we are talking strictly about shooting, the isosceles stance is likely a more stable position from which to shoot for most people.

As a state trooper, daily interactions with the public are routine. Although most of these encounters are uneventful, there are instances when someone might attempt to punch, push, or grab you. In such situations, maintaining a properly balanced stance is crucial for effectively countering these attacks. I naturally adopted this stance while shooting because law enforcement interactions can escalate from simple conversations to deadly force in less than a second.

While discussing concealed carry and self-defense, it is important to consider the dynamics of police interactions with individuals, such as during a roadside vehicle stop or pedestrian interaction. Many self-defense situations begin with some form of interaction—perhaps a discussion or verbal dispute—that can escalate into a physical confrontation involving pushing or punching. Therefore, it's crucial to be prepared for a physical altercation before a situation necessitates the use of a firearm.

Ultimately, it all depends on what you are training for and what you are trying to accomplish. You need to be comfortable shooting in whatever position you are in. An instructor can help you try out different positions, shooting stances, and variations.

Scanning and Assessing for Additional Threats

A comprehensive defensive shooting course will teach you how to effectively scan the area for additional threats if you ever need to use your firearm. For instance, from the ready position, you should turn your head from side to side to scan for any additional threats before reholstering your gun. Be mindful of your surroundings and ensure that your muzzle does not follow the movement of your head, as you do not want to inadvertently point your firearm at innocent bystanders.

Cover Versus Concealment

Always prioritize cover over concealment when possible. Earlier, we discussed cover versus concealment and the importance of identifying both while in public. A defensive shooting course should include shooting from cover.

You should know there are comprehensive courses available that focus specifically on defensive shooting. A qualified firearm instructor can provide guidance on the fundamentals and help you transition to effective defensive techniques for self-defense.

Being Mentally Prepared

Mental preparation is equally important and begins with developing a plan by considering various scenarios you might encounter. Practice visualization techniques, such as imagining yourself standing in line waiting to check out, as previously discussed. You can train for these scenarios using dry-fire devices or even your own unloaded gun in the safety and privacy of your own home. You can also practice home invasion scenarios.

Training under stress is essential because, during a high-stress encounter, you may experience sensory impairments such as hearing loss, tunnel vision, and temporary memory loss of incident details. Developing muscle memory through consistent practice of drawing, moving, and point shooting is vital for effective self-defense.

Having a defensive mindset means you may not have to use your firearm for self-defense. Consider the story of a woman named Jane, who was traveling on the New York City subway and found herself in a potentially dangerous situation. While she was waiting on the platform, despite the large crowd of people, she noticed a man acting suspiciously, his eyes darting around as he moved closer to her. Drawing from her training in self-defense and situational awareness, she discreetly shifted her position to keep the man in her peripheral vision while scanning for potential escape routes. She remembered a story from the book *The Gift of Fear: Surviving Signals that Protect Us from Violence* by Gavin de Becker, which emphasizes trusting your instincts and taking proactive measures when you sense danger.

Jane moved toward a group of people waiting for the train, ensuring she was not isolated. She then positioned herself near a transit officer, subtly signaling her concern by maintaining eye contact and moving closer. Her defensive mindset paid off; the suspicious man, realizing he had lost the element of surprise and couldn't easily target her, quickly changed his direction and disappeared into the crowd. This real-life scenario mirrors countless others where individuals, by staying alert and prepared, have avoided or mitigated danger, highlighting the importance of a defensive mindset in public spaces. This is a great example of the defensive mindset. Remember, the best way to win a confrontation is to avoid it!

With a solid foundation in crafting a defensive mindset, the next step is to elevate your defensive techniques. In the following chapter, we will delve into advanced strategies and practical skills that will further enhance your ability to protect yourself and others.

Chapter 6

ELEVATING DEFENSIVE
TECHNIQUES

Imagine a scenario where your safety is at risk, and your ability to defend yourself relies on split-second decisions and actions. The difference between successfully fending off a threat and becoming a victim often boils down to the effectiveness of your defensive techniques. In this chapter, we will unlock advanced strategies to elevate your defensive skills, ensuring you are prepared for any situation.

It's important for you to have self-defense skills—whether you carry a gun or not. If you do carry a gun, you need to be able to fight with your gun, either holstered or in one of the ready positions. In the academy, police officers are taught weapon-retention training. They engage in scenarios whereby other recruits try to disarm them while the officers are wearing their duty holsters. It's a very eye-opening experience. You should absolutely enroll in some type of weapon-retention training if you plan on carrying a gun.

We have already discussed the use of force and how a prosecutor will consider many factors in determining if your shooting was justified under the self-defense exception. Consider the real-life news story from 2023 of an armed employee who confronted a serial shoplifter:

Kevin Salas Madrid, 24, confronted the serial shoplifter and told him to leave the store. At that point, the shoplifter punched him in the face, knocking off Madrid's eyeglasses. Madrid then allegedly pulled out a gun and shot the shoplifter at least ten times, including several times when the shoplifter was on the ground. During his interview with police, "Kevin stated he had made the worst decision of his life." (Fox News, Online)

This incident is an example of how impulsive actions can lead to irreversible consequences.

When I read this story, my first thought was that the shooter had never been in a fight. He had probably never been punched or hit before in his life.

I believe Mike Tyson once said, "Everyone has a plan until they get punched in the mouth."

Before attending the state police academy, I dedicated many years to studying martial arts. During this time, we regularly engaged in sparring sessions and matches to put our skills to the test. I even competed in various tournaments for a period. At the academy, our training required that we demonstrate proficiency in self-defense techniques and boxing. Boxing was part of the self-defense training since, you are truly put to the fighting test during boxing. During one of the boxing sessions, I was paired with an opponent who managed to land a powerful punch, knocking me down. This occurred on more than one occasion.

Experiencing such a forceful punch that it knocks you down can be quite a shock initially. Individuals react differently to being struck; some may freeze, others might duck or cower, while some choose to fight back. In the academy, every aspect of your performance is under constant evaluation. Being knocked down taught me a valuable lesson: despite the painful surprise, I could still get up and continue the fight. It provided me with firsthand experience of what it's like to be punched by another person and how to gather the resilience to fight back, even while in pain.

Mr. Madrid obviously overreacted to the shock and pain of getting punched. He happened to be carrying a gun, and his impulsive decision, made in a moment of heightened emotion or stress, has had far-reaching and devastating consequences. I'm guessing if he'd had some self-defense training that involved fighting or sparring and had the experience of getting hit and knocked down, he may not have reacted the way he did. This underscores the importance of restraint and the need to consider the long-term repercussions of our actions.

Self-Defense and Training Schools

It is advisable to research self-defense training schools in your area to find one that best suits your needs. Ideally, you should speak to someone who currently attends or has previously attended the school to get their opinion on the training courses and an overall review of the institution. Once you select a school, enroll and commit to training.

Martial arts are a lifelong commitment to studying, practicing, and living by the philosophies and teachings. Nonetheless, many schools offer self-defense classes where you can learn basic leverage and body mechanics for close combat situations without spending years of training.

I recommend finding a school that can teach you some fundamental self-defense techniques that you can rely on if confronted. Learning and mastering one or two techniques that you feel confident using is a great starting point. As you become more comfortable and proficient, you can progress to more advanced techniques such as blocks, evasive footwork to neutralize an attacker, ground fighting, and escaping from grappling situations.

Other Non-Lethal/Less-Lethal Self-Defense Tools

There are a variety of defensive device options available to protect yourself other than firearms. Conducted energy devices, such as Tasers, are one such option. As with any weapon, check with your state or jurisdiction to find out what's legal before carrying it outside your home. In New Jersey, for example, current law only allows for carrying pepper spray, no more than 3/4 ounce, for self-defense outside your home. Of course, with a permit, you can carry a handgun, but there are many restrictions.

The State of NJ Attorney General's Office has said it will not prosecute conducted energy devices since a Supreme Court decision classified them as protected under the Second Amendment. However, you must meet certain requirements to legally possess one. Nonetheless, as of this date, the law has not changed to reflect allowing the carrying of conducted energy devices for self-defense, so I recommend not carrying one outside your home until the change in the law is made. You could also consult a licensed attorney for advice on carrying such devices in New Jersey.

Overall, however, Tasers or stun guns are an exceptional choice for self-defense. One popular variant is the contact stun gun, which offers the added benefit of providing a long-distance warning when activated. These devices are typically more affordable; however, they require direct physical contact, which means a close encounter with the assailant to be effective.

Taser offers a versatile model that doubles as a flashlight, making it a convenient and discreet option that can be easily carried in a purse or other bag.

Alternatively, you can opt for a model that shoots barbs up to 15 feet into your assailant. Longer distances are reserved for law enforcement officers. Once the barbs make contact, they can deliver up to 30 seconds of full lockup, giving you ample time to escape the situation. Some models also have contact stun for close encounters.

Pepper spray and pepper gel are highly effective tools for self-defense. You can carry a small container with you, keeping it ready as you walk to your vehicle, for example. The gel product is particularly advantageous as it significantly reduces the risk of blowback (when the irritant is blown back into your own face, causing you irritation), which is a common issue experienced by users of traditional spray products.

For home defense, consider purchasing a larger canister of pepper gel and mounting it in strategic locations around your home. Placing one near your fire extinguisher and another in your bedroom ensures you have quick and easy access during nighttime emergencies.

Pepper spray (or gel) is effective on most people. However, in my experience as a state trooper, I have seen it be less effective or not effective at all on people under the influence of drugs or alcohol since their pain sensitivity is blocked or suppressed. Many conducted energy devices that target neuromuscular incapacitation will still be effective even if the attacker is under the influence of drugs or alcohol since they cause involuntary muscle contractions.

Flashlights with strobe features are essential tools that everyone should carry, regardless of whether they have a firearm for self-defense. Flashlights are incredibly useful in low-light situations, and they come in various shapes and sizes to suit different needs. Some models offer USB charging capability, can fit on a keychain, and boast high lumen ratings for exceptional brightness that can temporarily blind an assailant.

One of the key advantages of a flashlight with a strobe function is its ability to be easily held in your hand while walking to your vehicle. If someone approaches too closely, you can activate the strobe light and shine it directly into their eyes, causing temporary blindness. This technique, often referred to as causing a *pause in combat*, can provide you with a crucial moment to either escape or access other self-defense tools like pepper gel or a concealed carry firearm, depending on your situation.

In summary, having the right flashlight with a strobe feature can significantly enhance your non-lethal self-defense options, making it a valuable addition to your personal safety arsenal.

Additionally, remember that everyday objects can be used as improvised weapons for self-defense if necessary. For instance, in an emergency at work, don't overlook the fire extinguisher on the wall or a stapler as potential tools for protection.

Tactical Use of Concealed Carry

Proper selection and placement of a holster for quick and safe access to your firearm is essential. With today's wide range of holster options, you can carry in many different configurations and locations on your body. However, be mindful that certain positions, such as an ankle holster, can be cumbersome and inefficient for accessibility. I have witnessed individuals at the range struggle to retrieve a gun from their ankle, getting caught on clothing, stumbling, or taking too long to access their firearm. However, although it might not be the ideal choice, it could be your only option depending on your attire.

As we discussed in Chapter 4, Concealed Carry Fundamentals, it is crucial to have a holster specifically designed for your gun model, one that secures your firearm to your body in an easily accessible manner and completely covers the trigger area. The placement of the holster on your body significantly impacts accessibility. Practicing various placement locations at the range with an instructor or range safety officer can help you develop a smooth and efficient draw technique under stress.

It is essential to practice weapon retention with your specific setup. Instructors typically provide training guns, often referred to as *blue guns* due to their color, which mimic the make and model of your firearm for training scenarios, including force-on-force exercises and weapon retention.

When engaging in physical force training (force-on-force), it is crucial to use a training device instead of your actual firearm for safety reasons. If you choose to use your real gun, ensure that all ammunition is removed from the firearm, double-check it, and have someone else verify that it is empty. Additionally, remove all live ammunition from the training area to maintain a safe environment.

If you have never experienced someone attempting to forcibly remove your gun from its holster, it can be a profoundly enlightening experience. I highly recommend that everyone who carries concealed participates in this type of training to better prepare for real-world scenarios.

Moreover, it's crucial to develop the ability to hit targets with precision and efficiency, even while on the move or from atypical stances. This practice prepares you for a wide range of real-life situations. Additionally, incorporating drills that involve shooting from behind cover or in low-light conditions can further enhance your readiness and adaptability in unpredictable environments.

Open Versus Concealed Carry

I should mention open carry since many states or jurisdictions now allow individuals to carry openly. Other states are more restrictive. For example, in New Jersey, you cannot carry openly unless you are an active-duty law enforcement officer, a qualified retired law enforcement officer carrying under the Retired Police Officer Permit (RPO) Program, or a licensed armed security officer carrying openly while working.

There are pros and cons to each option. Personally, I only carry concealed. Let me explain why I choose to do so and why I believe you should consider the same if you have the choice.

Open carry can make you a target. Criminals may try to neutralize you first to accomplish their goals. Alternatively, they might target you because you have a visible firearm, either as a challenge or to steal your gun. Open carry essentially broadcasts to everyone that you can fight back.

In the first scenario, imagine you're standing in line at a bank or store, and a criminal planning a robbery spots your firearm. They may decide to eliminate you first to remove the perceived threat.

In another scenario, a criminal without a gun might see your visible firearm as a challenge to obtain it from you. To these individuals, your open carry is an invitation.

The second scenario involves losing the element of surprise. If you're in a public place like a store or restaurant, and your firearm is not visible, no one knows you're armed and capable of defending yourself. This gives you a significant advantage. I prefer to keep this advantage; even when I was an active-duty trooper, I could carry openly off-duty but chose not to.

When you carry openly, it's like wearing a big sign that says, "I have a gun; come and get it or take me out first because I'm a threat to you."

Some might argue that open carry could deter criminals. While it might deter some, others may see it as a challenge.

There are exemptions, such as in New Jersey, where business owners may carry openly at their place of business without a permit, provided they legally own the firearm. However, this is different because they're usually behind a counter, aware of who enters their store, and maintaining situational awareness. This is not the same as standing in line at a supermarket or sitting in a restaurant with your back to the door and your gun visible.

Uniformed police officers utilize their visible presence and firearms as a form of deterrence, a concept known as constructive force. However, this visibility can also make them targets. Police officers accept this risk as an inherent part of their duties. Similarly, as a civilian who openly carries a firearm in public places, you must recognize that you are potentially making yourself a target, much like police officers sometimes are.

Therefore, I strongly recommend consistently carrying concealed to preserve the element of surprise and maintain a strategic advantage. But whatever you decide, it's crucial to remain vigilant of your surroundings and continuously practice situational awareness.

Hand-to-Hand Combat with Firearm Training

It's important to integrate firearm training with hand-to-hand combat for a comprehensive defense strategy.

While you may encounter situations that escalate immediately to deadly force, such as someone pointing a gun or a knife at you, many confrontations begin as physical altercations. Since you are carrying concealed, it is crucial to constantly be aware that there will always be at least one gun in any confrontation you face—your own. Therefore, avoidance is always the preferred strategy. While you can and should defend yourself, if necessary, the presence of a firearm on your person should make you reconsider engaging in any confrontation. If an altercation does occur, you must be capable of retaining your gun and physically defending yourself. If your attacker gains control of your firearm, they will possess a weapon they otherwise wouldn't have—yours.

Effective Concealment

Given the weight of this responsibility, understanding and adhering to essential principles of concealment is paramount. Effective concealment not only involves hiding your firearm but also ensuring it remains secure and accessible only to you. Additionally, blending into your environment without drawing attention to the fact that you are armed is crucial. By mastering these principles, you enhance your safety and the safety of those around you, minimizing the likelihood of a confrontation escalating to deadly force.

In July 2013, George Zimmerman, a neighborhood watch volunteer, fatally shot Trayvon Martin, an unarmed 17-year-old, in Sanford, Florida. Mr. Zimmerman had a concealed carry permit and was armed with a 9 mm pistol. The confrontation began as a physical altercation after Zimmerman followed Martin, suspecting him of suspicious activity. Even though police advised Zimmerman to remain in his vehicle, he still approached Martin, leading to a struggle. During the fight, Zimmerman claimed Martin attacked him, and fearing for his life, he used his firearm, resulting in Martin's death.

This tragic incident highlights the critical importance of avoiding confrontations when carrying a concealed gun. Zimmerman's decision to engage Martin instead of waiting for law enforcement escalated the situation to deadly force. Concealed carry holders must prioritize de-escalation and awareness, understanding that their firearm introduces a potentially lethal element into any conflict. Effective concealment, along with the ability to defend oneself without resorting to firearms, is essential in preventing such tragic outcomes, ensuring the safety of both the carrier and the community.

Active Intruder / Shooter

When we talk about an active intruder or active shooter, many people have heard the phrase *Run, Hide, Fight.* We will break this down as to what it means in terms of practicality.

If you find yourself in one of these situations and you have a concealed carry gun, you will most likely be featured on the news as the next good guy with a gun for stopping the attack. However, many people do not carry concealed, and we will address what you can do if you're one of these individuals.

Unfortunately, there's no one-size-fits-all or template of what to do in every situation because every situation is different. However, if you follow these three rules, your chances of surviving an encounter with an active shooter greatly increase.

Run, Hide, Fight, and not in any order, as these can change based on your situation.

Let's break it down:

Rule #1: Run

This rule is simple: if you hear gunshots, you run.

It seems clear enough, but in the chaos of hearing gunshots and people screaming, you might not immediately think, "I need to get out." But that should be the first thing you do if possible. However, don't just run indiscriminately. You may think the shots are coming from the left when, in fact, they are coming from the right. Sounds can play tricks on our minds, so stop for a second and try to figure out where the shots are coming from.

Some people have been known to run toward the shooter, thinking the gunshot sounds were coming from the opposite direction. Also, you may see a crowd of people running. You don't necessarily want to join them. Active shooters often target large groups of people because there are many potential victims in one spot. Their goal, as horrific as it is, is to shoot and kill as many people as possible as quickly as possible. They know that once the police or someone with a firearm arrives, it's over for them. Typically, those who target unarmed individuals are cowards and understand that once someone with equal firepower arrives, they are finished.

So, you may want to be in a smaller group or alone to increase your chances of survival. If you are running, try to use short sprints, and if you're running down a long hallway or large open room, use a zig-zag pattern, as that will make it much more difficult for the shooter to hit you. A moving target is significantly harder to hit than a stationary one. When running, move from cover to cover or concealment to concealment.

Now, if you're a student at school, schools have protocols in place, and your best bet may be lockdown. Many schools have highly secure classrooms, and when the doors lock, it's very difficult for anyone to get inside. So, if you're a student, follow your school's protocol or a teacher's or school official's instructions if you're in school. But if there aren't any teachers or school officials around, follow these rules.

Rule #2: If You Can't Leave, Then Hide

If you're in school, this typically means a lockdown. During a lock-down, students are secured in a classroom or another safe room and instructed to remain silent and out of sight until the police neutralize the threat. We discussed concealment and cover previously, but let's have a quick recap.

Remember, **concealment** means you are hidden from view but not protected from bullets. For instance, hiding behind a thin wall or a coat hanging on a rack provides concealment but won't stop a bullet. In contrast, **cover** means hiding behind something that can stop a bullet, such as a solid wood desk, a car's engine block, or a concrete wall. Ideally, you should seek cover, but in emergencies, you may have to settle for concealment.

Concealment can also involve hiding in plain sight, such as "playing dead." However, this carries risks, as the shooter might still target individuals or bodies on the ground. Assess your situation and options carefully. Sometimes, playing dead might be your best choice, but it's a personal decision. My preferred choice is to fight, which I will discuss in the next section.

It's essential to identify potential hiding spots beforehand. When-ever I go for coffee or grocery shopping, I consider the exits and identify good hiding spots, noting whether they offer cover or con-cealment. I mentioned before that this is my thought process while standing in line at Home Depot or Target: "What if someone starts shooting? What would I do? Where would I go?" Think about these scenarios during your daily routines.

By pre-planning, you'll have a spot in mind if something hap-pens, making it easier to execute your plan. Most of us frequent the same places regularly, so take the time to assess these locations. Next time you're there, ask yourself, "If someone started shooting right now, where would I go? What would I do? Where could I hide? Would that be cover or concealment?"

When choosing hiding spots, avoid dead ends like bathrooms or supply rooms without exits. Movies often show characters running upstairs to escape a gunman, but this is usually a poor choice unless there's an alternate exit, like a fire escape. Always try to take cover in a room you can barricade and still have another exit, if possible. Consider these spots beforehand, maybe at your workplace.

If you find a suitable spot, barricade the door once inside. Avoid standing directly in front of the door, as shooters often fire through doors. Place heavy objects like furniture in front of the door and stack them linearly to the opposite wall if possible.

Remember to silence your cell phone and lock any other entrances to your room. Stay quiet, make the room appear empty by keeping it dark, and take cover inside. Stay very low or even high in the room, considering the possibility of shots being fired through the door. Ensure you are clear of potential bullet paths.

Rule #3: Fight

If you can't leave and you can't hide, it is time to fight.

Regardless of your size, strength, age, or physical condition, find something you can use to defend yourself. Remember, *you are fighting for your life,* so make every effort count. Whether it's a stapler, a bottle, a piece of wood, or a fire extinguisher, use whatever you can to throw or hit your attacker. If you have never been in a physical confrontation before, consider taking a self-defense course to boost your confidence and improve your abilities.

If you are with other people, quickly formulate a plan to neutralize the shooter. For example, one person could target the attacker's body or legs, while another goes for the gun. Take down the attacker by any means necessary, gain control of the weapon, and, if necessary, use it against them. Secure the attacker until help arrives.

If the attacker is close and pauses, perhaps to reload (since magazines only hold a limited number of bullets), seize that moment to attack. Formulate a plan and stick to it.

Regarding the wounded, remember that you must stop the threat before you can help them. The goal of an active shooter is to cause as much death, fear, and destruction as possible in the shortest amount of time. Neutralize the threat before attempting to assist anyone who is injured.

This is why current police training emphasizes engaging and entering a structure with an active shooter immediately upon arrival, even if alone. There is no waiting for backup, as the goal is to stop the shooter as quickly as possible. Police officers are trained to head directly toward the shooter to neutralize them.

Remember, you are fighting for your life. Your adrenaline will be increased, making it difficult to control your movements, so do your best. Your primary objectives are to create pain, disarm the attacker, and take them down. If there are enough people, hold the attacker in place until the police arrive. Do whatever you need to do to survive.

Many people remember one quiet afternoon in 2019 when a gunman entered a synagogue in Poway, California, during a Passover service. The situation was dire, and lives were at stake. Oscar Stewart, a U.S. Army veteran, was among the congregants. Quickly assessing the danger, Stewart formulated a plan with another attendee, Jonathan Morales, an off-duty Border Patrol agent. Stewart charged at the gunman, shouting and creating a distraction. At the same time, Morales drew his firearm and targeted the attacker, causing him to flee. He was apprehended later.

This is a great example of how a quick, coordinated action can neutralize a shooter before more harm can be done. Between Stewart's bravery and Morales's precision, I'm sure many lives were saved that day. This real-life event underscores the importance of immediate, decisive action in crisis situations. By working together and targeting the attacker strategically, Stewart and Morales were able to gain control of the situation and stop the attacker until law enforcement arrived and apprehended him. Their heroism stands as a powerful testament to the profound impact that swift decision-making and cohesive teamwork can have in critical life-or-death situations.

But remember: Every situation is different, and you must assess what is happening in front of you and consider your personal abilities to determine your actions. However, if you keep the three rules in mind during an active shooter situation, you will have a plan to survive.

Now that you've learned advanced techniques to elevate your defensive skills, it's time to focus on developing an unbreakable sense of confidence. In the next chapter, we will explore strategies and mindset shifts that will help you achieve unshakable confidence in your ability to protect yourself and your loved ones.

Would you like to see my YouTube videos on surviving an active shooter incident? They are on my Book Bonuses Page, along with many other great resources: https://mtgsafety.com/

Chapter 7

ACHIEVING UNSHAKABLE CONFIDENCE

Have you ever wondered what separates a confident defender from one who is riddled with doubt? The answer lies in mastering the inner game of self-assurance, a skill cultivated through practice, knowledge, and mindset. Consider the story of Nelson Mandela, who, despite facing 27 years of imprisonment, emerged as a symbol of hope and resilience for South Africa. Mandela's unwavering confidence was not natural; it was honed through years of introspection, reading, and a strong belief in justice. He once said, "I learned that courage was not the absence of fear, but the triumph over it." This mindset enabled him to lead his nation out of apartheid and into a new era of equality.

Similarly, in the excruciating hours of the Tham Luang cave rescue in 2018, the world witnessed what separates a confident defender from one riddled with doubt. British cave divers Rick Stanton and John Volanthen epitomized unshakable confidence as they navigated the hazardous, flooded cave system to reach 12 young boys and their soccer coach trapped inside. Their self-assurance was not inherent but was cultivated through years of practice, knowledge, and a resilient mindset. Every dive, every challenge faced underwater, had prepared them for this moment. Their survival mindset enabled them to stay calm and focused, ultimately leading to the miraculous rescue of all 13 individuals.

We've all seen the iconic photographs of the D-Day landings, capturing the moment when over 150,000 Allied soldiers stormed the beaches of Normandy on June 6, 1944. This bold assault shattered the formidable German coastal defenses and paved the way for the liberation of Western Europe from the Nazi regime. One of these images hangs on my wall with a caption that reads "Courage." Beneath it, a powerful message is inscribed: "Bravery doesn't mean you aren't scared. It means you go anyway." I'm sure many of those soldiers were undoubtedly terrified on that fateful day, yet they found the strength to do what was necessary.

This mindset of facing fear head-on is not confined to historic battles; it is a principle that can be applied to any self-defense situation where your life is at risk. Embracing courage means acknowledging your fear but choosing to act regardless, ensuring your safety and the safety of others around you.

Building Mental Resilience

Understanding the importance of a positive mindset is crucial. Confidence begins with believing in your abilities and the training you have undergone. By practicing visualization techniques, you can mentally prepare yourself for high-stress scenarios, imagining yourself successfully navigating through them.

It's essential to develop coping strategies to manage stress and anxiety, such as through breathing exercises and meditation. Take, for instance, the employee who confronted the serial shoplifter. While having fighting experience might have been advantageous, the stress and anxiety he felt after being punched were likely overwhelming, causing him to overreact.

Establish practical objectives by dividing your goals into manageable steps. This method not only sustains your enthusiasm but also allows you to monitor your advancements efficiently. By celebrating each small victory, you can maintain a positive outlook and stay on course toward your goal. Additionally, regular reflection on your progress can provide valuable insights, helping you to adjust your strategies as needed for continuous improvement.

Rather than viewing an event as a setback, consider it an invaluable opportunity to gain knowledge and develop your psychological resilience. Each challenge you encounter presents a unique chance to grow and improve. Embrace these moments to reflect on what went wrong and how you can adapt in the future. By shifting your perspective, you transform obstacles into stepping stones toward greater achievements.

Pilots are trained to adopt this mindset with every approach to landing, takeoff, and flying in general. Given that weather conditions and aircraft configurations are always changing, each approach and departure requires different inputs and adjustments. By adopting the principle that "a good pilot is always learning," you can instill a sense that constant improvement is possible. This mindset encourages you to continually evaluate your performance and make the necessary adjustments for future success.

Enhancing Physical Preparedness

Regular training will provide consistent practice with your concealed carry pistol and enhance muscle memory and reaction times. Likewise, maintaining a level of fitness that supports quick movements and endurance during high-stress situations is essential.

Engaging in scenario-based drills is crucial for simulating real-world situations, as it helps build familiarity and reduces hesitation during actual events. For instance, if the employee who confronted the serial shoplifter had previously experienced a controlled

fight, he would have at least been familiar with the sensation of being struck.

As a police aviator, I was required to attend annual training using
a sophisticated flight simulator that was an exact replica of the aircraft
we were flying. This advanced, full-motion simulator could be pro-
grammed by the flight instructors to mimic virtually any real-world
scenario, allowing them to evaluate our reactions and responses. The
realism was such that the FAA certified it for official flight testing and
evaluation. This simulator provided a safe environment to practice
emergencies that would otherwise be too dangerous to simulate in a
real aircraft, such as shutting down one or both engines or deploying
floats for an emergency water landing.

Likewise, during my time as a state police recruit and later as
a sworn state trooper, I participated in numerous scenario-based
training programs. These programs, often based on actual real-life
events, provided a valuable platform to develop quick and effective
reactions under stress.

Being physically prepared also involves having the right equipment. It's crucial to ensure your concealed carry gear is comfortable,
easily accessible, and dependable. Regularly check your gear for any
signs of wear or damage. The last thing you want is for someone to
be able to grab and pull your firearm from your body because you
missed a crack or defect in the holster, and it failed when stressed.
Additionally, consider rotating your gear periodically to ensure even
wear, and practice drawing your firearm under various conditions to
stay proficient and ready for any situation.

Continual education is a must and includes staying updated on
the latest self-defense techniques and laws to maintain a well-rounded
skill set. As previously mentioned, many states, including New Jersey,
have passed laws restricting the carrying of guns by lawful citizens
since the landmark U.S. Supreme Court *NYSRPA v. Bruen* decision.
There are many pending lawsuits challenging parts or all of these
laws, and sometimes, it can get confusing as to what the current law

allows for concealed carry while these cases move through the court system. One way to stay up to date on laws is to find an organization that monitors Second Amendment challenges and sign up, donate, or both to receive email alerts when significant changes occur. You can also reach out to your local police department, state police, state attorney general's office, or a licensed attorney for current information.

Cultivating Situational Awareness

We've talked about the importance of situational awareness, which is essentially the practice of being acutely aware of your surroundings to identify potential threats and unusual activities. This involves staying vigilant by continuously observing your environment and establishing a baseline of what is considered normal behavior in your specific setting. This baseline enables you to quickly notice any deviations.

It's crucial to trust your gut feelings. If something doesn't feel right, it's important to acknowledge it and be ready to take appropriate action. Don't dismiss your instincts by thinking you're just being overly cautious.

In our modern world, distractions are abundant, particularly from electronic devices. Notice how often people are engrossed in their smartphones while walking, waiting at crosswalks, or sitting on benches. This makes them potential targets for criminals who are always on the lookout for distracted individuals.

In 2013, Antoinette Tuff, an elementary school bookkeeper in Atlanta, Georgia, demonstrated exceptional situational awareness that ultimately saved countless lives. On August 20, a gunman entered the school's front office armed with an AK-47 and 500 rounds of ammunition. Despite the immediate and obvious danger, Tuff remained calm and observant, quickly developing a baseline of the gunman's behavior and intentions.

As the situation unfolded, Tuff trusted her instincts and engaged the gunman in conversation, recognizing anomalies in his behavior that suggested he might be talked down. Although he had a gun, something convinced her she could reach him. She used empathetic communication and shared personal stories to humanize herself and establish a connection. Her alertness and ability to maintain focus during a chaotic scene allowed her to understand the immediate threat and respond effectively. In a world where distractions are ever-increasing, Tuff's unwavering attention to her environment and the unfolding situation was crucial.

Ultimately, Tuff's situational awareness and calm demeanor persuaded the gunman to put down his rifle and surrender to authorities, preventing a potentially catastrophic event. Her actions underscore the importance of staying alert, trusting one's instincts, and avoiding distractions to respond appropriately in critical situations. This remarkable event stands as the only school active shooter incident in the United States that concluded without any fatalities or injuries to students, faculty, parents, or the gunman himself. Her natural and remarkably effective negotiation skills on that day earned widespread praise from seasoned hostage negotiators, law enforcement professionals, and community leaders. By regularly practicing observation and maintaining situational awareness, individuals can better protect themselves and others in times of crisis.

Now that you've learned the secrets to achieving unshakable confidence, it's time to wrap up your journey. In conclusion, we will summarize the key takeaways and provide final thoughts to ensure you are fully prepared to defend confidently.

CONCLUSION

As we conclude our exploration of mastering situational awareness and the responsible use of concealed carry, it's essential to recognize that this is merely the beginning of an ongoing journey.

Maintaining safety is not always straightforward or convenient. It requires a careful balance between vigilance and daily convenience. Cultivate strong safety practices and remain consistently alert to your environment. Remember, survival is rooted in a proactive mindset!

Moreover, continuous learning and regular practice are key. Engage in ongoing training, stay informed about new safety techniques, and adapt to evolving situations. Your dedication to safety and preparedness will not only protect you but also those around you. Stay committed, stay aware, and embrace the mindset of a survivor.

Carrying a concealed gun for protection is just another tool for self-defense. If you decide that carrying a gun is not the right choice for you, there are numerous non-lethal or less-than-lethal device options available. Alternatively, if you choose to carry a firearm to protect yourself and your loved ones, it is imperative to fully comprehend the responsibilities and implications associated with carrying a gun for protection.

Carrying a firearm for self-defense is a significant decision that comes with immense responsibility. You must possess the emotional maturity and appropriate mindset to use your gun strictly as a last resort. Additionally, you must be capable of de-escalating your use of force if the situation changes.

Furthermore, you must be prepared for the potential consequences if you ever have to use your gun for self-defense. These include possible criminal or civil ramifications (or both), psychological issues stemming from processing the event and your actions, and potential relationship difficulties, especially if a spouse or partner was not supportive of you carrying a gun in the first place.

Always remember that in any confrontation you are involved in, there will be at least one gun present—yours. Therefore, it should be your top priority to de-escalate or exit the encounter before it escalates into a situation requiring deadly force, if possible. While you absolutely can and should defend yourself if threatened, there are many situations you can walk away from, especially when carrying a firearm.

You must be proficient in fighting with your firearm and ensuring that it cannot be taken from you. Creating a deadly force situation due to an inability to retain your self-defense firearm is unacceptable.

As a newcomer to concealed carry, it is essential to recognize that the best way to build comfort and confidence is through frequent carrying and continuous training. I vividly remember my initial experiences with carrying a firearm, particularly during off-duty hours. Adjusting to this new responsibility required some changes to my wardrobe, and, initially, I was always acutely aware of the gun attached to my body. Over time, however, carrying a gun became as natural as carrying my wallet, keys, or cell phone—I barely noticed it anymore. Even today, I periodically check its position on my body to confirm it's still there. But while your brain will eventually adapt and make the firearm feel like just another part of your daily carry, never forget the immense responsibility that comes with it.

In addition, regular training sessions will help reinforce muscle memory, making you more adept at handling your firearm. Engaging in advanced training that includes stressful scenarios can significantly boost your confidence. However, it's crucial to approach training as an ongoing process rather than a one-time or occasional activity. Even police officers, despite their ongoing training, face similar challenges when confronted with dangerous situations. Consistent practice and preparedness are key to effective concealed carry.

In her book, *The Unthinkable: Who Survives When Disaster Strikes and Why*, Amanda Ripley emphasizes that the critical difference between surviving a crisis and succumbing to it often lies in preparation and understanding how the brain responds to fear. Through interviews with police officers who have faced life-and-death situations, Ripley discovered that even highly trained individuals experience the same emotions and reactions as those without training. However, the crucial distinction is that trained officers' muscle memory frequently takes over, allowing them to navigate and survive dangerous circumstances. This principle also applies to civilians: the more information or training a person has, the less likely they are to shut down during an emergency or crisis.

Ripley also emphasizes the crucial importance of being attuned to your senses when they signal that something is wrong or out of place. It is imperative to heed these sensory warnings and take immediate, decisive action. She discusses various levels of fear and highlights how many people are often paralyzed by shock at the onset of a critical incident. This paralysis often prompts first responders to issue loud commands or instructions to get people moving to safety. During a presentation, she recounted how Captain Chesley "Sully" Sullenberger, who famously landed an airliner on the Hudson River, initially thought to himself, "This can't be happening," after losing both engines due to striking a flock of geese.

Clearly, Captain Sullenberger overcame the initial shock phase and was able to draw upon his years of training and experience to safely land the commercial airliner on the Hudson River without any casualties.

Ongoing learning and regular practice are crucial. Participate in continual training, keep up to date with the latest safety techniques, and be ready to adapt to changing situations. Your commitment to safety and preparedness not only safeguards you but also those around you. Stay dedicated, remain vigilant, and adopt the mindset of a warrior to survive.

Finally, consider the broader implications of your actions. Your preparedness and situational awareness can contribute to a safer community. Stay informed about local laws and regulations, and always prioritize responsible behavior. By doing so, you set an example for others and help foster a culture of safety and responsibility.

Stay safe!

Your Next Step to Confidence and Safety

Thank you for completing *Defend Confidently*! Your journey to self-defense mastery doesn't end here. As a token of appreciation, we're offering you exclusive bonuses to further enhance your skills and confidence. Visit https://mtgsafety.com to unlock your free resources. You've come this far—now take the next step toward fully protecting yourself and those you love!

Bibliography/Citations

Gavin De Becker, *The Gift of Fear: Survival Signals That Protect Us from Violence* (New York: Little, Brown and Company, 1997).

Dan Millman, *Way of The Peaceful Warrior* (Belvedere Tiburon, Calif.: H. J. Kramer Inc., 2000).

Amanda Ripley, *The Unthinkable: Who Survives When Disaster Strikes and Why* (New York: Harmony, 2024).

Encyclopedia Britannica website

https://www.britannica.com/science/amygdala

RAINN website

https://rainn.org/statistics/scope-problem

Fox News website

https://www.foxnews.com/us/arizona-family-dollar-employee-charged-murder-firing-10-shots-shoplifter-punched

www.ingramcontent.com/pod-product-compliance
Ingram Content Group UK Ltd.
Pitfield, Milton Keynes, MK11 3LW, UK
UKHW021437050126
9904UKWH00037B/1329